Mitchell Symons was born in 1957 in London and educated at Mill Hill School and the LSE, where he studied law. Since leaving BBC TV, where he was a researcher and then a director, he has worked as a writer, broadcaster and journalist. He was a principal writer of early editions of the board game Trivial Pursuit and has devised many television formats. He is also the author of more than thirty books, and currently writes a weekly column for the *Sunday Express*.

www.kidsatrandomhouse.co.uk

Also by Mitchell Symons

WHY EATING BOGEYS IS GOOD FOR YOU

HOW MUCH POO DOES AN ELEPHANT DO?

WHY DO FARTS SMELL LIKE ROTTEN EGGS?

WHY DOES EAR WAX TASTE SO GROSS?

WHY YOU NEED A PASSPORT
WHEN YOU'RE GOING TO PUKE

DO IGLOOS HAVE LOOS?

MITCHELL SYMONS

How to avoid a
wombat's
BUM

. . . and other fascinating facts!

RED FOX

HOW TO AVOID A WOMBAT'S BUM
A RED FOX BOOK 978 1 862 30183 2

First published in Great Britain by Doubleday,
an imprint of Random House Children's Books
A Random House Group Company

Doubleday edition published 2006

Red Fox edition published 2008
This edition published 2010

5 7 9 10 8 6

Text copyright © Mitchell Symons, 2006
Illustrations copyright © Sara Freeman, 2006
Insides designed by Fiona Andreanelli

The Random House Group Limited supports the Forest Stewardship
Council (FSC), the leading international forest certification organization.
All our titles that are printed on Greenpeace-approved FSC-certified paper
carry the FSC logo. Our paper procurement policy can be found at
www.rbooks.co.uk/environment.

Mixed Sources
Product group from well-managed
forests and other controlled sources
www.fsc.org Cert no. TT-COC-2139
© 1996 Forest Stewardship Council

Set in Tyfa and Spleeny Decaf

Red Fox Books are published by Random House Children's Books,
61–63 Uxbridge Road, London W5 5SA

www.**kids**at**random**house.co.uk

Addresses for companies within The Random House Group Limited
can be found at: www.randomhouse.co.uk/offices.htm

THE RANDOM HOUSE GROUP Limited Reg. No. 954009

A CIP catalogue record for this book is available from the British Library.

Printed in the UK by CPI Bookmarque, Croydon, CR0 4TD

To children everywhere – but especially mine

ACKNOWLEDGEMENTS

I had a lot of fun compiling this book. Most of the facts were collected and stored over the past twenty years but I also took material from the Internet – especially in the sections Creepy Crawlies, The Human Condition, Fish, Geography, Birds, History, Animals and Science.

I also had a lot of help from a lot of people – principally (in alphabetic order): Fiona Andreanelli, Luigi Bonomi, Penny Chorlton, Annie Eaton, Emma Eldridge, Sara Freeman, Shannon Park and Mari Roberts.

In addition, I'd also like to thank the following people for their help, contributions and/or support: Gilly Adams, Jeremy Beadle, Marcus Berkmann, Jonathan Fingerhut, Jenny Garrison, Tricia Martin, Bryn Musson, Sophie Nelson, Nicholas Ridge, Simon Rose, Charlie Symons, Jack Symons, Louise Symons, David Thomas, Martin Townsend, Rob Woolley and Doug Young.

Last, but not least, I'd like to thank the pupils of Malmesbury Primary School in Bow, East London – especially Meryem, Asmeena, Meiyyu, Shahena, Chay, Charlie, Rajul, Imran, Akbar and the awesome Lamisa – who road-tested the book and told us what worked (and, just as valuable, what didn't). If I've missed anyone out, then please know that – as with any mistakes in the book – it's entirely down to my own stupidity.

Mitchell Symons, 2006
www.mitchellsymons.co.uk

WHERE CAN I FIND THINGS ABOUT . . . ?

Amphibians 230
Animals 14, 54, 64, 66, 73, 120, 130, 134, 148, 162, 174, 216, 220, 224, 270, 289
Around the World 8, 36, 90, 91, 116, 142, 155, 156, 159, 171, 174, 214, 227, 232, 234, 255, 282, 284
Astronomy 252
Beds and Sleep 86
Before the Age of 10 172, 244
Birds 42, 74, 76
Books 8, 122, 123, 170, 178, 179, 197
Celebrities 9, 10, 48, 61, 67, 75, 93, 123, 132, 169, 184, 185, 188, 192, 193, 196, 200, 201, 202, 204, 235, 240, 242, 244, 281, 288, 291, 292, 293, 304
Creepy Crawlies 18, 102, 160, 174, 210, 268
Dates 108, 121, 285
Film 106, 190
First Things 1, 5, 6
Fish 68, 69, 174, 259, 278
Food 115, 144, 152, 273
Geography 34, 136, 166, 246
History 44, 58, 124, 126, 127, 182, 183, 208, 222, 260

Human Body 21, 28, 29, 101, 128
Last Things 306, 311, 312
Marine Mammals 118, 258, 278
Music 296, 308
Numbers 80, 250, 256
Plants 104, 114
Pure Trivia 38, 50, 110, 164, 212, 264, 274, 300, 302
Reptiles 92, 94, 96, 174
Science 30, 219
Sport 33, 40, 65, 83, 88, 112, 168, 193, 198, 204, 226, 228, 240, 290, 291
Strange and Stupid Things! 16, 84, 176, 180, 205, 218, 236, 286, 287, 297, 300
Television 113
The Human Condition 24, 62
Toilet Facts 22, 206, 207, 304, 305
Toys and Games 46, 140, 177, 294
Weather 146
Wombats 289
Words 12, 72, 98, 138, 151, 199, 248, 251, 296, 298, 299, 311

FIRST THINGS

1. The first ready-to-eat breakfast cereal was Shredded Wheat in 1893 (it beat Kellogg's Corn Flakes by just five years).

2. **The first photograph of the moon was taken in 1839 (by Louis Daguerre) but the details were not clear. J. W. Draper took the first recognizable photograph a year later.**

3. The first man to fly over the North Pole – and indeed the South Pole – was called Dickie Byrd.

4. **Gustav Mahler composed his first piece of music at the age of four, Sergei Prokofiev composed his first piece of music aged five and Wolfgang Mozart was eight when he composed his first symphony.**

5. The first member of the Royal Family ever to leave home for a haircut was the Queen. It was in Malta back in the days when she was a princess.

6. **The first personal computer, the Apple II, went on sale in 1977.**

☐ Everton was the first British football club to introduce a stripe down the side of players' shorts.

☐ **The first ice lolly dates back to 1923 when lemonade salesman Frank Epperson left a glass of lemonade with a spoon in it on a windowsill one very cold night: the next morning, the ice lolly was born.**

☐ The first song to be sung in outer space was *Happy Birthday* – sung by the *Apollo IX* astronauts on 8 March 1969.

☐ **The London Underground system was first used in 1863.**

☐ The first ever organized Christmas Day swim in the freezing cold Serpentine in London's Hyde Park took place in 1864.

☐ **Pitcairn Airlines was the first airline to provide sick bags (in 1922).**

- The first sport to have a world championship was billiards in 1873.

- The first in-flight movie was shown on a Lufthansa flight on 6 April 1925.

- Austria was the first country to use postcards.

- The first product to have a bar code was Wrigley's chewing gum.

- The first words spoken on the telephone by its inventor, Alexander Graham Bell, were: 'Watson, come here, I need you.'

- The first toothbrush was invented in China in 1498.

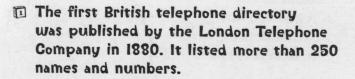

- The first British telephone directory was published by the London Telephone Company in 1880. It listed more than 250 names and numbers.

- Captain Cook was the first man to set foot on every continent (except Antarctica).

- Beethoven's Fifth was the first symphony to include trombones.

1. Ice-cream cones were first served at the 1904 World's Fair in St Louis, United States of America.

1. Bingo was first played in 1888.

1. Spectacles were first worn in Italy in about 1285.

1. The first Internet domain name to be registered was symbolics.com in March 1985.

1. The first man-made object to break the sound barrier was a whip.

MOUNT EVEREST FIRSTS

First ascent: 29 May 1953 by Edmund Hillary and Tenzing Norgay.

First recorded deaths: seven Sherpas in an avalanche in 1922.

First person to reach the summit twice: Nawang Gombu Sherpa on 20 May 1965.

First woman to reach the summit: Junko Tabei on 16 May 1975.

First ascent without bottled oxygen: Peter Habeler and Reinhold Messner on 8 May 1978.

First winter ascent: Krzysztof Wielicki on 17 February 1980.

First blind person to reach the summit: Erik Weihenmayer on 25 May 2001.

BEGINNINGS

A newborn kangaroo is small enough to fit in a teaspoon.

Babies born in May are on average 200 grams heavier than babies born in other months.

From fertilization to birth, a baby's weight increases 5,000 million times.

One mouse can give birth to 100 babies in a year.

Kiwis lay the largest eggs (relative to body size) of any bird.

Numbering houses in London streets began only in 1764.

When a polar-bear cub is born, it can't see or hear for the first month.

The first novel written on a typewriter was *The Adventures of Tom Sawyer*.

Screwdrivers were first used to help knights put on armour.

The smoke detector was invented in 1969.

The wristwatch was invented in 1904 by Louis Cartier.

Leonardo da Vinci invented an alarm clock that woke the sleeper by rubbing his feet.

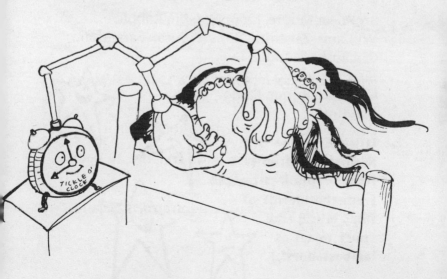

THE CHILDREN'S LAUREATE

2009-2011 Anthony Browne

2007-2009 Michael Rosen

2005-2007 Jacqueline Wilson

2003-2005 Michael Morpurgo

2001-2003 Anne Fine

1999-2001 Quentin Blake

UNICEF AMBASSADORS

Sir Roger Moore, Liam Neeson, Robbie Williams, Zinédine Zidane, Susan Sarandon, Samantha Mumba, Luis Figo, Francesco Totti, Claudia Schiffer, Paolo Maldini

(UNICEF – the United Nations Children's Fund – appoints people from the worlds of film, music and sport to act as 'ambassadors'.)

WHAT THEIR FATHERS DID FOR A LIVING

David Beckham	kitchen fitter
Jamie Oliver	publican
Jim Carrey	accountant
Christina Aguilera	US army sergeant
Emma Bunton	milkman
Wayne Rooney	labourer
Anna Kournikova	wrestler
Ben Affleck	social worker
Christian Bale	airline pilot
Ryan Giggs	rugby league professional
Sacha Baron Cohen ('Ali G')	menswear-shop owner
Jennifer Lopez	computer specialist at Guardian Insurance in NYC
Leonardo DiCaprio	comic-book dealer
Tom Cruise	electrical engineer
Will Smith	refrigeration engineer
Gareth Gates	postman
J. K. Rowling	engineer
Reese Witherspoon	doctor

PARENTS

Kerry Katona, Kelly Holmes, David Blaine, Eminem, Lance Armstrong, Sir Charlie Chaplin, Bill Clinton, Eric Clapton, Naomi Campbell and Mike Tyson never knew their fathers.

The fathers of Queen Latifah, Ross Kemp, Arnold Schwarzenegger and Eddie Murphy were all policemen.

The mothers of Oscar Wilde and Franklin D. Roosevelt dressed their sons as girls for the first few years of their lives.

David Beckham's mother was a hairdresser.

Jeremy Clarkson's mother made her fortune from Paddington Bear merchandise.

Ryan Giggs (Wilson), Kevin Spacey (Fowler), Beck Hansen (Campbell) and Patsy Palmer (Harris) all use their mother's last name instead of their father's.

When Sir Michael Caine was a child, his mother pasted his ears to his head to stop them sticking out.

'My mother loved children – she would have given anything if I had been one' **Groucho Marx**

'My mum was a great feminist and always said, "Hold your head high – no matter what happens. It's fine, as long as you know you've conducted yourself properly"' Nicole Kidman

'When I was growing up, the biggest influence in my life was my mother. She made great sacrifices to send me to private school and I will always be grateful for that' **Naomi Campbell**

WORDS

'Stewardesses' is the longest word typed with only the left hand.

The only 15-letter word that does not repeat a letter is 'uncopyrightable'.

Shakespeare invented more than 1,700 words, including 'assassination' and 'bump'.

Hull City is the only British football team that hasn't got any letters you can fill in with a pen.

The ball on top of a flagpole is called the 'truck'.

Zenith, tariff, sherbet, algebra, carafe, coffee, syrup, cotton, mattress and alcohol are all words derived from Arabic.

'Knightsbridge' is the place name with the most consonants in a row.

Food that's spat out is called 'chanking'.

IOU doesn't stand for 'I owe you'. It stands for 'I owe unto'.

1,000 words make up 90 per cent of all writing.

A 'clue' originally meant a ball of thread. This is why you 'unravel the clues' of a mystery.

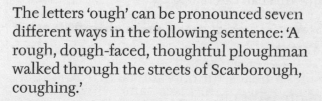

No word in the English language rhymes with orange, silver, month, pint or diamond.

Queue is the only word in the English language to be pronounced the same way even if the last four letters are removed.

The name 'jeep' came from the abbreviation 'GP', used in the army for general-purpose vehicle.

The letters 'ough' can be pronounced seven different ways in the following sentence: 'A rough, dough-faced, thoughtful ploughman walked through the streets of Scarborough, coughing.'

Alice in Wonderland **author, Lewis Carroll, invented the word 'chortle' – a combination of 'chuckle' and 'snort'.**

'Taramasalata' (a type of Greek pâté) and 'Galatasaray' (name of a Turkish football club) each have an 'a' for every other letter.

ANIMALS

Most dinosaurs were no bigger than chickens.

A mouse has more bones than a human: mouse 225, human 206.

A newborn panda is smaller than a mouse.

The armadillo is the only animal – apart from man – that can catch leprosy.

A beaver can chop down more than 200 trees in a year.

Besides humans, the only animal that can suffer sunburn is the pig.

A skunk will not bite and throw its scent at the same time.

A rabbit takes about 18 naps a day.

Giant pandas can eat 38 kilograms of bamboo a day.

A dog can suffer from tonsillitis, but not appendicitis. It doesn't have an appendix.

A monkey was once tried and convicted for smoking a cigarette in Indiana.

At full speed, a cheetah takes eight-metre strides.

Koalas have no natural predators.

A rodent's teeth never stop growing.

A donkey will sink in quicksand but a mule won't.

Tigers have striped skin, not just striped fur.

Male monkeys go bald in much the same way that men do.

Polar bears can smell a human being from 20 miles away.

Polar bears cover their black noses with their paws for better camouflage.

THE NAMES OF THINGS YOU DIDN'T KNOW HAD NAMES

Aglet: the metal or plastic covering on the end of a shoelace.

Armsate: the hole in a shirt or a jumper through which you put your hand and arm.

Diastema: a gap between your teeth.

Ferrule: the metal band on the top of a pencil that holds the rubber in place.

Fillip: the technical term for snapping your fingers.

 Keeper: the loop on a belt that holds the end in place after it has passed through the buckle.

Mucophagy: the medical term for 'snot-eating', the consumption of the nasal mucus obtained from nose-picking.

Obdormition: when an arm or a leg goes to 'sleep' as a result of numbness caused by pressure on a nerve.

Ophyron: the space between your eyebrows.

Peen: on a hammer, the end opposite the striking face.

Pips: the little bumps on the surface of a table-tennis bat.

Purlicue: the space between the extended thumb and index finger.

Rasceta: the creases on the inside of your wrist.

Rowel: the revolving star on the back of a cowboy's spurs.

Tragus: the little lump of flesh just in front of the ear.

Ullage: the empty space in a bottle between the surface of the liquid and the bottle top.

Zarf: a holder for a hot cup or mug.

CREEPY CRAWLIES

🦋 A queen bee lays about 1,500 eggs a day.

🦋 **A scorpion could withstand 200 times more nuclear radiation than a human could.**

🦋 The colour of head lice can depend on the hair colour of the person carrying them.

🦋 **The sound made by bees, mosquitoes and other buzzing insects comes from their rapidly moving wings.**

🦋 Monarch butterflies migrate beween southern Canada and central Mexico, a distance of 2,500 miles. They weigh 0.5 gram, travel at 20 miles per hour and reach altitudes of 3,000 metres.

🦋 **A moth has no stomach.**

🦋 The rarest breed of millipede has approximately 750 legs.

🦋 **Flies take off backwards.**

🦋 A caterpillar has twelve eyes.

The silk of a spider's web is the strongest natural fibre known to man. Its ability to bear weight is greater than that of steel (relative to its size).

Mosquito repellents don't repel mosquitoes but rather prevent the mosquitoes from knowing you are there by blocking their sensors.

Termites will eat your house twice as fast if you play them loud music.

The silkworm, *Bombix mori*, is the only truly domesticated insect. The adult moths are so tame they can barely fly and must be fed by hand.

There are more insects in one square mile of rural land than there are human beings on Earth.

Spiders cannot be farmed to produce silk commercially – in the way that silkworms can – because they are too antisocial.

❋ **A leech has 32 brains.**

❋ A greenfly born on Sunday can be a grandparent by Wednesday.

❋ **There are over 1,800 known species of flea.**

❋ The longest earthworm ever found was 6.7 metres long.

❋ **A female mosquito can produce 150,000,000 young in one year.**

❋ Some ribbon worms will eat bits of themselves if they can't find any food.

❋ **A bee produces only 1/12 of a teaspoon of honey in its life.**

❋ Bees flap their wings 11,400 times a minute.

❋ **Crickets 'hear' through their knees.**

❋ A cockroach can live for several weeks after being decapitated.

❋ **The silkworm has 11 brains. But it uses only five of them.**

HUMAN BONES

The human body grows the equivalent of a new skeleton every seven years.

Adult humans have 206 bones. At birth, an infant has 350 bones. As the child grows, many bones fuse together.

A quarter of the 206 bones in the human body are in the feet.

Babies are born without kneecaps. Kneecaps develop when the child is between two and six years old.

It's impossible for you to lick your own elbow.

The hardest bone in the human body is the jawbone.

Your skull is made up of 29 different bones.

TOILET FACTS

Sir John Harington (1561–1612) invented the toilet for Queen Elizabeth I after she'd banned him from her court for circulating smutty stories. She allowed him to return to court. Sir John's toilet did the job but there were unpleasant side effects, such as the smell.

The Victorian plumber Thomas Crapper perfected the system we all know and use: the siphon flush, which, by drawing water uphill through a sealed cistern, is both effective and hygienic.

The most impossible item to flush is a ping-pong ball.

***Psycho* was the first Hollywood film that showed a toilet flushing – and was the subject of many complaints.**

The first time women and men used separate toilets was in 1739 at a Paris ball.

The idea of separate cubicles for toilets is a relatively modern invention; the Romans, for example, sat down together in large groups.

In Victorian times, loo seats were always made of wood: the well-to-do sat on mahogany or walnut while the poor put up with untreated white pine.

Soft toilet paper was sold for the first time in Britain in 1947 and was only available in Harrods.

The first toilet air-freshener was a pomegranate stuffed with cloves.

The Victorians gave their loos names such as Cascade, Optimus, Alerto, Pluvius, Deluge, Tornado, Aquarius, Niagara, Planetas and the Subito.

The town council of Cheltenham Spa once voted to replace the words 'Men' and 'Women' on their public toilets with 'Ladies' and 'Gentlemen' in order 'to attract a better class of person'.

In the Middle Ages, sewage from public latrines ran directly into the river or the sea.

THE HUMAN CONDITION

People who live in the city have longer, thicker nose hairs than people who live in the country (because they breathe more polluted air).

In your whole life, you will sleep for about 220,000 hours – or just over 25 years.

Your stomach produces a new layer of mucus every two weeks so that it doesn't digest itself.

Children have more taste buds than adults.

Right-handed people tend to scratch with their left hand, and vice-versa.

If you yelled for eight years, seven months and six days, you would have produced enough sound energy to heat enough water for one cup of tea.

Babies can breathe and swallow at the same time until they're six months old.

Rubbing the groove between your lips and your nose in a circular fashion is said to help get rid of cravings for sweets and chocolates.

Humans are the only animals to sleep on their backs.

When we blush, our stomach lining also turns red.

We shed about 20 kilograms of dead skin in a lifetime.

Your tongueprint is as unique as your fingerprints.

A newborn baby cries, on average, for 113 minutes a day.

The most common disease in the world is tooth decay.

You inhale thousands of your own skin flakes each day.

One in every 2,000 babies is born with a tooth.

Smiling is easier than frowning. We use 43 muscles to frown; we use 17 muscles to smile.

The acid in the human stomach is strong enough to dissolve a nail.

The digestive tract is more than nine metres long.

According to medical experts, babies dream in the womb.

The fastest-moving muscle in your body is the one that opens and closes the eyelid.

Our head is a quarter of our total length at birth, but an eighth of our total length by the time we reach adulthood.

The most sensitive nerves in the body are at the base of the spine.

Every human spent about half an hour as a single cell.

The thumbnail grows the slowest; the middle nail the fastest.

In 24 hours, you breathe about 23,040 times.

The sound you hear when you put a shell to your ear is not the sea but blood flowing through your head.

More people are allergic to cow's milk than to any other food.

Children everywhere in the world play hide-and-seek.

Our hearing is less sharp after eating too much.

It takes about seven minutes to fall asleep.

We use 54 muscles every time we step forward.

A person will die from a total lack of sleep more quickly than they will from starvation.

At 90 degrees below zero your breath will freeze in mid-air and fall to the ground.

EYES

- Eyes are made up of more than two million working parts.

- The average person's field of vision is an angle of 200 degrees.

- The eye muscles are the most active muscles in the whole body.

- As a child grows, the body part that grows least is the eye. While the rest of an adult body is 20 times bigger than it was at birth, the eye is only three and a quarter times bigger.

- There are over 100 million light-sensitive cells in the retina of the eye.

- Vision requires more brain power than the other four senses (hearing, taste, feeling and smell).

- The colour red can promote hunger, which is why so many fast-food establishments use red in their logos and décor.

- Your eyes will be closed for about 30 minutes a day because of blinking.

- Our eyes don't freeze in very cold weather because of the salt in our tears.

THE HEART

♥ The human heart has enough pumping pressure to squirt blood nine metres.

♥ A newborn baby's heart beats twice as fast as an adult's.

♥ The average person's heart beats 36 million times a year.

♥ The right lung takes in more air than the left, because the left lung is smaller to make room for the heart.

♥ The human heart pumps about one million barrels of blood during an average lifetime.

SCIENCE

❀ Surgeons who spend three hours a week playing video games make fewer mistakes during operations.

❀ **The microwave was invented after a researcher walked past a radar tube and a chocolate bar melted in his pocket.**

❀ Cut an onion in half, rub it on the sole of your foot and an hour later you'll taste onion in your mouth.

❀ **Britney Spears and Anna Kournikova have both had computer viruses named after them.**

❀ Grapes explode when you put them in the microwave.

❀ **The first blood transfusion was in 1668. The doctors used sheep's blood and the patient died. The first successful transfusion – using human blood this time – was in 1818.**

❀ If you slowly pour a handful of salt into a totally full glass of water, it will not overflow. In fact, the water level will go down.

✷ **Waves break when their height reaches more than 7/10ths of the total depth of the water.**

✷ X-ray technology has shown that there are three different versions of the *Mona Lisa* under the one that's visible.

✷ **Because of gravity, it is impossible for a mountain to be higher than 15,000 metres.**

✷ Hot water freezes more quickly than cold water.

✷ **At the deepest point of the ocean, an iron ball would take more than an hour to sink to the ocean floor.**

✷ Sterling silver contains 7.5 per cent copper.

✷ **Only 4 per cent of the energy put out by an ordinary light bulb is light. The rest is heat.**

✷ If you went unprotected into space, you would explode before you suffocated.

✷ **The cracks in breaking glass move at speeds of up to 3,000 miles per hour.**

✼ Methane gas can often be seen bubbling up in ponds. It is produced by decomposing plants and animals in the mud at the bottom.

✼ No matter how high or low it flies, an aeroplane's shadow is always the same size.

✼ The holes in fly swatters are there to reduce air resistance. For the same reason, you should open your fingers when trying to kill mosquitoes between the palms of your hands.

✼ Because of the rotation of the Earth, you can throw something further if you throw it west.

✼ In a scientific study, children were told to imagine they were wearing warm gloves, then the temperature of their fingertips was measured. Their hands had warmed up as though they had been wearing gloves for real.

THE ONLY COUNTRIES TO HAVE WON THE WIMBLEDON MEN'S SINGLES TITLE

COUNTRY	WINS	THE MOST RECENT
UK	35	Fred Perry in 1936
USA	33	Pete Sampras in 2000
Australia	21	Lleyton Hewitt in 2002
France	7	Yvon Petra in 1946
Sweden	7	Stefan Edberg in 1990
Switzerland	16	Roger Federer in 2009
New Zealand	4	Tony Wilding in 1913
Germany	4	Michael Stich in 1991
Spain	2	Rafael Nadal in 2008
Czechoslovakia	1	Jan Kodes in 1973
Holland	1	Richard Krajicek in 1996
Croatia	1	Goran Ivanisevic in 2001

GEOGRAPHY

Tasmania has the cleanest air in the inhabited world.

The furthest point from any ocean would be in China.

There are no public toilets in Peru.

The Red Sea is not red.

China uses 45 billion chopsticks per year.

The Pacific Ocean covers 28 per cent of the Earth's surface.

The poorest country in the world is Mozambique. (Switzerland is the richest.)

At their nearest point, Russia and America are less than four kilometres apart.

Alaska is the most northern, western and eastern state in the United States; it also has the highest latitude, and is big enough to hold the 21 smallest states.

Mongolia is the largest landlocked country.

Norway's total coastline is longer than that of the United States, although its landmass is 27 times smaller.

The East Alligator river in Australia's Northern Territory harbours crocodiles, not alligators.

La Paz in Bolivia is so high above sea level there is barely enough oxygen in the air to support a fire.

Antarctic means 'opposite the Arctic'.

Fewer than 1 per cent of the Caribbean Islands are inhabited.

The volume of water in the Amazon river is greater than the combined volume of the next eight largest rivers in the world.

There is no point in England more than 75 miles from the sea.

Sahara means 'desert' in Arabic.

The Angel Falls in Venezuela are nearly 20 times taller than Niagara Falls.

AROUND THE WORLD

The letter 'O' in Irish surnames means 'grandson of'.

Rome has more homeless cats per square mile than any other city in the world.

Churches in Malta show two different times to 'confuse the devil'.

Mango is the bestselling fruit in the world, and India is the biggest grower.

Japan has 24 recorded instances of people receiving serious or fatal skull fractures while bowing to each other in the traditional greeting.

The largest McDonald's in the world is in Beijing, China.

At one time it was against the law to slam car doors in Switzerland.

Antarctica is the only continent without snakes or reptiles.

● In Lima, Peru, there is a large brass statue of Winnie-the-Pooh – even though it's Paddington Bear who came from Peru.

● **Panama hats come from Ecuador.**

● Bulgarians eat more yogurt than any other nationality.

● **Until 1984, Belgians had to choose their children's names from a list of 1,500 drawn up in the days of Napoleon.**

● The province of Alberta in Canada has been completely free of rats since 1905.

● **Aircraft are not allowed to fly over the Taj Mahal.**

● The harmonica is the world's most popular musical instrument to play.

● **There are about 5,000 different languages in the world.**

● More than a hundred cars can drive side by side on the Monumental Axis in Brazil, the world's widest road.

PURE TRIVIA

Diet Coke was invented in 1982. However, in 1379, a Mr and Mrs Coke of Yorkshire named their daughter 'Diot' (a short form of Dionisia, the modern-day name Denise).

111,111,111 x 111,111,111 = 12,345,678,987,654,321.

Where the stones are of equal size, a flawless emerald is worth more than a flawless diamond.

Pearls melt in vinegar.

20 per cent of all the people in the whole history of mankind who have lived beyond the age of 65 are alive today.

The buttons on a man's jacket cuff were originally intended to stop menservants from wiping their noses on the sleeves of their uniforms.

An alternative title that was considered for the show *Friends* was *Insomnia Café*.

At 2 minutes past 8 o'clock in the evening of 20 February 2002, the time was, for sixty seconds only, in perfect symmetry: 2002, 2002, 2002. Or, to be more precise: 20.02, 20/02/2002. At 12 minutes past 9 o'clock in the evening of 21 December 2112, the same symmetry will exist: 2112, 2112, 2112. Or: 21.12, 21/12/2112. (But none of us will live long enough to see it.)

In Victorian times fire engines were pulled by horses. The horses were stabled on the ground floor of the fire stations, which had circular staircases to stop them trotting upstairs.

Pollen lasts for ever.

The South Pole has no sun for 182 days each year.

Catherine the Great, Empress of Russia in the 18th century, relaxed by being tickled.

If Barbie – whose full name is Barbara Millicent Roberts – were lifesize, she would have a neck twice the length of a normal human's neck.

SOCCER FANZINES WITH FUNNY NAMES

Linesman You're Rubbish	**Aberystwyth Town**
Only the Lonely	**Airdrie**
Shots in the Dark	**Aldershot**
The Ugly Duckling	**Aylesbury United**
Revenge of the Killer Penguin	**Bath City**
4,000 Holes	**Blackburn Rovers**
Our Flag's Been to Wembley	**Braintree Town**
Beesotted	**Brentford**
And Smith Must Score	**Brighton & Hove Albion**
Addickted	**Charlton Athletic**
Super Dario Land	**Crewe Alexandra**
Mission Impossible	**Darlington**
The Gibbering Clairvoyant	**Dumbarton**
It's Half Past Four ... And We're 2–0 Down	**Dundee**
One Team in Dundee	**Dundee United**
Away From the Numbers	**East Fife**
We'll Score Again!	**Exeter City**
Sing When We're Fishing	**Grimsby Town**
Crying Time Again	**Hamilton Academicals**
Monkey Business	**Hartlepool Town**
Still Mustn't Grumble	**Hearts**
From Hull to Eternity	**Hull City**
To Elland Back	**Leeds United**

The Keeper Looks Like Elvis	**Kidderminster Harriers**
Where's the Money Gone?	**Leicester City**
Another Wasted Corner	**Liverpool**
Mad As a Hatter	**Luton Town**
Dial M for Merthyr	**Merthyr Tydfil**
No One Likes Us	**Millwall**
Waiting for the Great Leap Forward	**Motherwell**
Once Upon a Tyne	**Newcastle United**
What a Load of Cobblers	**Northampton Town**
Frattonise	**Portsmouth**
The Memoirs of Seth Bottomley	**Port Vale**
Exceedingly Good Pies	**Rochdale**
Get a Grip, Ref!	**Scunthorpe United**
The Ugly Inside	**Southampton**
A View to a Kiln	**Stoke City**
It's the Hope I Can't Stand!	**Sunderland**
Nobody Will Ever Know	**Swansea City**
Friday Night Fever	**Tranmere Rovers**
Moving Swiftly On …	**Walsall**
Flippin' Heck, Ref, That Was a Foul Surely!	**Waterlooville**
Winning Isn't Everything	**Welling United**
Over Land and Sea	**West Ham and Partick Thistle**
The Sheeping Giant	**Wrexham**
She Fell Over	**Yeovil Town**

BIRDS

The albatross can glide on air currents for several days at a time.

Owls are the only birds that can see the colour blue.

The owl can't move its eyes, but it is the only creature that can turn its head in a complete circle.

The longest recorded chicken flight is 13 seconds.

Female canaries can't sing.

The most common bird in the world is the starling.

The golden eagle can spot a rabbit from nearly two miles away.

The penguin is the only bird that walks upright. It is also the only bird that can swim but not fly.

Pigeons are the only birds that can drink water without having to raise their heads to swallow. Other birds need gravity to help them swallow.

Australian lyrebirds mimic what they hear, and can reproduce the sound of anything from a car alarm to an electric chainsaw.

Parrots, most famous of all talking birds, can have a vocabulary of up to 20 words.

Pet parrots can eat most of the food we eat, with the exception of chocolate and avocados, which are highly toxic for parrots.

The kea parrot in New Zealand likes to eat the rubber strips that line car windows.

Male cockatoos can be taught to speak, but females can only chirp and sing.

A sparrow's brain is 4 per cent of its total body weight (ours is 2 per cent).

Homing pigeons use roads in their route-finding. Some pigeons even fly around roundabouts before choosing the exit that leads them home.

HISTORY

The Egyptians thought it was good luck to enter a house left foot first.

The song 'Chopsticks' was written in 1877 by Euphemia Allen, aged 16. She said that the correct way to play it was to chop the keys with the hands turned sideways.

Abdul Kassem Ismael, the Grand Vizier of Persia in the 10th century, carried his library with him wherever he went. The 117,000 volumes were carried in alphabetical order by 400 camels.

Cleopatra wrote a book on cosmetics. One of the ingredients was burnt mice.

Virginia Woolf and Lewis Carroll wrote their books standing up.

Richard the Lionheart, King of England for 10 years in the 11th century, only spent a few months in England.

Between 1839 and 1855, Nicaragua had 396 different rulers.

The Wright brothers' first flight was shorter than the wingspan of a 747.

Ancient Egyptians slept on pillows of stone.

Mexico once had three presidents in one day.

In ancient Greece, tossing an apple to a girl was a traditional proposal of marriage. Catching it meant she accepted.

Leonardo da Vinci could write with one hand and draw with the other at the same time.

George I, King of England from 1714 to 1727, was German and couldn't speak a word of English.

Louis XIV of France took just three baths in his lifetime (and he had to be forced into taking those).

Bagpipes were invented in Iran, then brought to Scotland by the Romans.

George Washington's false teeth were carved from hippopotamus ivory and cow's teeth and fixed together with metal springs.

Moby Dick sold 50 copies during its writer Herman Melville's lifetime.

THE BRITISH ASSOCIATION OF TOY RETAILERS' TOY OF THE YEAR

2009	Go Go Hamsters
2008	Ben 10 Action Figures 10" and 15"
2007	In The Night Garden Blanket Time Igglepiggle
2006	Dr Who Cyberman Mask
2005	Tamagotchi Connexion
2004	Robosapien
2002/2003	Beyblades
2001/2002	Bionicle by Lego
2000/2001	Teksta
1999/2000	Furby Babies
1998	Furby
1997	Teletubbies
1996	Barbie
1995	POGS
1994	Power Rangers
1993	Thunderbirds Tracey Island

1992	WWF Wrestlers
1991	Nintendo Game Boy
1990	Teenage Mutant Ninja Turtles
1989/1988/1987	Sylvanian Families
1986/1985	Transformers (Optimus Prime)
1984	Masters of the Universe
1983/1982	Star Wars toys
1981/1980	Rubik's Cube
1979	Legoland Space kits
1978	Combine Harvester (Britains)
1977	Playmobil Playpeople
1976	Peter Powell kites
1975	Lego Basic set
1974	Lego Family set
1973	Mastermind – board game
1972	Plasticraft modelling kits
1971	Katie Kopykat writing doll
1970	Sindy
1969	Hot Wheels Cars
1968	Sindy

SINGULAR PEOPLE

- Jack Nicholson was in detention every day for a whole school year.

- Mariah Carey's vocal range spans five octaves.

- Florence Nightingale used to travel everywhere with a pet owl in her pocket.

- David Beckham is superstitious and salutes magpies.

- Melissa Joan Hart can recite the mathematical expression 'pi' to 400 decimal places.

- When he was a teenager, Colin Farrell put Smarties under his pillow to bring Marilyn Monroe back from the dead.

- The writer Jacqueline Wilson had *Jackie* magazine named after her.

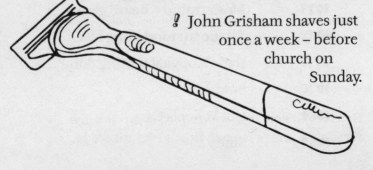

- John Grisham shaves just once a week – before church on Sunday.

! Robbie Williams made a cameo appearance in 1995 in *EastEnders* making a telephone call from a payphone in the Queen Vic.

! Richard Gere never swears. If a visitor swears in his home, he asks them to leave.

! Nicolas Cage ate a live cockroach for *Vampire's Kiss*.

! Gordon Brown won a *Daily Express* competition for a vision of Britain in the year 2000 when he was 21.

! Albert Einstein couldn't speak properly until he was nine.

! Anna Kournikova hasn't cut her waist-length hair since she was seven.

! Jennifer Lopez takes her own sheets when she stays at a hotel.

! Robson Green has a category-four licence for doing professional fireworks displays.

PURE TRIVIA

The man who invented FM radio was Edwin Armstrong. The first men to use FM radio to communicate with Earth from the Moon's surface were Edwin 'Buzz' Aldrin and Neil Armstrong.

The average ratio of yellow kernels to white kernels in a bag of popcorn is 9:1.

Pepper was sold in individual grains during Elizabethan times.

The name of the character behind bars in the Monopoly board game is Jake the Jailbird.

A full moon always rises at sunset.

A full moon is nine times brighter than a half moon.

Jodie Foster was mauled by a lion when she was a child.

In Belgium, there is a strawberry museum.

Velcro was invented by a Swiss man who noticed the way burrs attached themselves to clothing.

Native speakers of Japanese learn Spanish more easily than they learn English.

The distress term 'Mayday' comes from the French term 'm'aidez' meaning 'help me'.

Strawberries have more vitamin C than oranges.

In Disney's *Fantasia*, the Sorcerer's name is Yensid, which is Disney backwards.

Roosters can't crow if their necks aren't fully extended.

The three largest landowners in England are the Queen, the Church of England and Trinity College, Cambridge.

All gondolas in Venice have to be painted black unless they belong to a high official.

Studies indicate that weightlifters working out in blue gyms can handle heavier weights.

Frosties' Tony the Tiger turned 50 in 2005.

Charles Lindbergh took just four sandwiches with him on his famous transatlantic flight.

The sport with the highest ratio of officials to participants is tennis. A singles match should have 13:10 line umpires, one net official, one foot-fault official and a chair umpire.

The shortest intercontinental commercial flight is from Gibraltar (Europe) to Tangier (Africa). The distance is 34 miles and the flight takes 20 minutes.

The US has more bagpipe bands than Scotland.

Flamingo tongues were a delicacy in ancient Rome.

The YKK on a zip stands for Yoshida Kogyo Kabushibibaisha, the world's largest zip manufacturer.

Before 1800 there was no such thing as separate shoes for left and right feet.

Offered a new pen to try, 97 per cent of people will write their own name.

Given sufficient amounts of chocolate as encouragement and reward, pigs can master video game skills.

A coward was originally a boy who took care of cows.

Cows can be identified by their noseprints.

In 1517, the *Mona Lisa* was bought by King Francis I of France to hang in a bathroom.

Cows give more milk when they listen to music.

There are 10 million bacteria in a litre of milk. That's the same number of bacteria as there are people in Greece.

In the 1994 World Cup the entire Bulgarian team had surnames ending with the letters 'ov'.

Donald Duck has a sister called Dumbella.

Snow White's sister is called Rose Red.

In 1933, Mickey Mouse got 800,000 fan letters.

Watermelon is a vegetable.

It is physically impossible for pigs to look up into the sky.

ANIMALS

Australia, New Zealand, Uruguay, Syria and Bolivia all have more sheep than people.

Sheep will not drink from running water.

The pupils in goats' and sheep's eyes are rectangular.

Baby opossum are so tiny at birth that an entire litter would fit into a tablespoon.

By the age of six months, a baby pig will have increased its weight 7,000 times.

When the first duck-billed platypus arrived at the British Museum, the curators tried to pull its beak off. They thought it was a fake.

Gibbons communicate through high-pitched songs that can be heard over a distance of miles.

Hippopotamuses kill more people in Africa than lions, elephants and water buffalo combined, usually by trampling on them.

You can smell the unpleasant odour of a skunk from a mile away.

The tuatara lizard of New Zealand has three eyes – two that are positioned normally and an extra one on top of its head.

The black bear has a blue tongue.

The two best-known cat noises are roaring and purring. But only four kinds of cat can roar – lions, leopards, tigers and jaguars – and none of them can purr.

An adult lion's roar is so loud, it can be heard up to five miles away.

Lions sleep for up to 20 hours a day.

Lions cannot roar until they reach the age of two.

The lioness does more than 90 per cent of the hunting. The male lion is lazy.

A lion's muzzle is unique – no two lions have the same pattern of whiskers.

The kinkajou, which belongs to the same family as the raccoon, has a tail that is twice the length of its body. At night it wraps itself up in its tail to sleep.

Rabbits and parrots can both see behind themselves without turning their head.

When hippopotamuses get upset, their sweat turns red.

A hippopotamus can open its mouth wide enough to fit a child inside.

A hippopotamus can bite a crocodile in half.

A hippopotamus's stomach is three metres long.

80 per cent of the noise a hippopotamus makes is done underwater.

A hippopotamus can outrun a man.

A hippopotamus is born underwater.

The skin of a hippopotamus is nearly bulletproof.

Besides humans, the only animal that can stand on its head is the elephant.

The elephant is the only mammal that can't jump.

Giraffes can't cough.

Brand-new baby giraffes are 1.8 metres tall and weigh 90 kilograms.

Giraffes rarely sleep more than 20 minutes a day.

A giraffe can clean its ears with its 50cm tongue.

We have the same number of bones in our neck as a giraffe does.

When a giraffe is born, it has to fall about two metres to the ground.

The reindeer is the only female animal with antlers.

HISTORY

No one knows where the composer Wolfgang Amadeus Mozart is buried.

From 1807 till 1821, the capital of Portugal was moved to Rio de Janeiro, Brazil, while Portugal was fighting France in the Napoleonic Wars.

The Toltecs, 7th-century Mexicans, went into battle with wooden swords so as not to kill their enemies.

Roman emperor Caligula once decided to go to war against the god of the sea, Poseidon. He ordered his soldiers to throw their spears into the water. He also made his horse a senator.

In the 1500s, one out of 25 coffins was found to have scratch marks on the inside.

The people of East Anglia used to mummify cats and place them in the walls of their homes to ward off evil spirits.

Armoured knights raised their visors to identify themselves when they rode past their king. This custom has become the modern military salute.

People didn't always say hello when they answered the phone. When the first regular phone service was established in 1878, people said 'Ahoy'.

AHOY!

King Richard II died in 1400. A hole was left in the side of his tomb so people could touch his royal head, but 376 years later someone stole his jawbone.

Between the two World Wars, France had 40 different governments.

Instant coffee has been around since the 18th century.

Albert Einstein was once offered the presidency of Israel. He declined, saying he had no head for problems.

In 18th-century Britain, you could take out insurance against going to hell.

In Egypt in the late 19th century, mummies were used as fuel, since wood and coal were scarce but mummies were plentiful.

The river Nile has frozen over twice – once in the 9th century, and again in the 11th century.

In ancient Egypt, if a patient died during an operation, the surgeon's hands were cut off.

In ancient China, doctors were paid only if the patient stayed well. If the patient's health got worse, the doctor had to pay the patient.

In ancient Egypt, when a cat died, its owner shaved off his eyebrows to show his grief.

In 1830, King Louis XIX ruled France for 15 minutes.

India was the richest country in the world until the time of the British invasion in the early 17th century.

Leprosy is the world's oldest known disease, dating back to 1350 BC.

The imperial throne of Japan has been occupied by the same family for the last 1,300 years.

It cost $7 million to build the _Titanic_ and $200 million to make a film about it.

Playing cards that were issued to British pilots in the Second World War could be soaked in water and unfolded to reveal a map in the event of capture.

In England in the 17th century, families had an average of 13 children.

PEOPLE WHO HAVE BEEN HONOURED WITH UNIVERSITY DOCTORATES

Tony Blair	Northumbria
Pierce Brosnan	Dublin Institute of Technology
Sir Alex Ferguson	Robert Gordon University in Aberdeen
Sir David Attenborough	Bristol
Sir Sean Connery	Heriot-Watt
Matt Damon	Harvard
Robert De Niro	New York
J. K. Rowling	D. Litt, Exeter

THE HUMAN CONDITION

There are twice as many left-handed boys as there are left-handed girls.

Girls smile more than boys do.

Girls have more taste buds than boys.

Boys get hiccups more often than girls do.

Girls can hear better than boys.

More boys than girls are born during the day; more girls are born at night.

Girls can detect smell better than boys.

Over a 12-day period, your body generates a whole new set of taste buds.

The strongest muscle in the body is the tongue.

The foot is the part of the body most often bitten by insects.

Humans can distinguish between 3,000 and 10,000 different smells.

The size of your foot is approximately the size of your forearm.

Fingernails grow four times faster than toenails.

Your feet are bigger in the afternoon than at any other time of day.

In one day you will take about 18,000 steps.

The tongue is the fastest-healing part of the body.

One person in two billion will live to be 116 or older.

The average person is a quarter of an inch taller at night. (You shrink again during the day!)

A sneeze travels at 600 miles per hour.

The most sensitive finger is the forefinger.

A nail grows from base to tip in about six months.

Everyone sprays microscopic saliva droplets into the air when they talk, about two or three droplets for each word.

Hair is made from the same substance as fingernails.

CATS

Cats have over 100 vocal sounds; dogs have about 10.

The last of a cat's senses to develop is its sight.

A cat uses its whiskers to determine if a space is big enough to squeeze through.

The ferret was domesticated 500 years before the cat. The female ferret is called a jill.

Cats have better memories than dogs. Tests conducted by an American university concluded that a dog remembers things for five minutes, while a cat can remember things for 16 hours.

Cats can't survive on a vegetarian diet.

The cheetah is the only cat that can't retract its claws.

Cats can hear ultrasound.

A cat's jaws can't move sideways.

Cats can't taste sweet food.

A cat has 32 muscles in each ear.

ALL THE BRITISH FORMULA 1 WORLD MOTOR-RACING CHAMPIONS

Mike Hawthorn	1958
Graham Hill	1962 and 1968
Jim Clark	1963 and 1965
John Surtees	1964
Jackie Stewart	1969, 1971 and 1973
James Hunt	1976
Nigel Mansell	1992
Damon Hill	1996
Lewis Hamilton	2008
Jenson Button	2009

CAMELS

Thinking that its parents were a camel and a leopard, Europeans once called this animal a 'camelopard'. Today, we know it as the giraffe.

The hump of a starving camel may flop over and hang down the side of its body because the fat in it has been used up.

Giraffes can live without water for longer than camels can.

Camels chew in a figure-of-eight pattern.

A rat can last longer without water than a camel can.

Camels have three eyelids to protect their eyes from sand.

Despite the hump, a camel's backbone is as straight as a horse's.

UNUSUAL MIDDLE NAMES

Mel	COLUMCILLE	Gibson
Joseph	ALBERIC	Fiennes
Geri	ESTOLLE	Halliwell
Leonardo	WILHELM	DiCaprio
Russell	IRA	Crowe
John	MARWOOD	Cleese
Robson	GOLIGHTLY	Green
Lawrence	BRUNO NERO	Dallaglio
Hugh	MUNGO	Grant
Ben	GEZA	Affleck
Emile	IVANHOE	Heskey
Robbie	MAXIMILIAN	Williams
Richard	TIFFANY	Gere
Courteney	BASS	Cox
Billie	PAUL	Piper

GOLDFISH

Goldfish are the most popular pets.

Goldfish can suffer motion sickness.

**A goldfish has a memory span
of three seconds.**

The oldest goldfish ever known was 41.

**Goldfish kept in a darkened room eventually
turn white.**

A pregnant goldfish is called a twit.

FISH

- **Starfish don't have brains.**

- The starfish is the only creature that can turn its stomach inside out.

- **The catfish has over 27,000 taste buds – more than any other creature.**

- Some sharks swim in a figure of eight when threatened.

- **The male rather than the female seahorse carries the eggs.**

- Fish have eyelids.

- **When seahorses want to stay in one place, they wrap their tails round some seaweed.**

- 'Fry' is the term for young fish that are newly hatched.

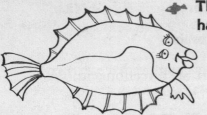

The flounder, a flat fish, has both eyes on one side of its body.

The herring is the most widely eaten fish in the world.

The largest species of seahorse is 20 centimetres tall.

Giant Antarctic cod grow up to two metres long, weigh up to 90 kilograms and live for up to 30 years.

Most tropical marine fish could survive in a tank filled with human blood.

An elastic stomach permits the deep-sea anglerfish to swallow prey larger than itself.

Atlantic salmon can leap 4.5 metres into the air.

A male catfish keeps the eggs of his young in his mouth until they are ready to hatch. After they have been born, if they are in any danger, the father once again opens his huge mouth and lets the youngsters hide inside.

The female starfish produces two million eggs a year, of which 99 per cent are eaten by other fish.

A starfish can move in any direction without having to turn since it has no front or back.

The mudskipper is a fish that can walk on land.

The gurnard, a fish found in Florida, grunts when a thunderstorm is brewing, and is said to be more reliable than weather-forecasters.

The lantern fish has a glowing spot on its head that would be bright enough to read by.

Fish that live more than half a mile below the surface of the sea don't have eyes.

Tuna swim at a steady rate of nine miles per hour until they die – they never stop moving and would suffocate if they did.

ANAGRAMS

'Eleven plus two' is an anagram of 'Twelve plus one'.

NO, I DECLINE	Celine Dion
BEGS HUGE ROW	George W. Bush
BRAVO! I'M ACE THICK	Victoria Beckham
BLAME, COMPLAIN	Naomi Campbell
I AM ONLY A LASS	Alyssa Milano
DOCILE OR PARANOID	Leonardo DiCaprio
OLD WEST ACTION	Clint Eastwood
HIM ALL SPOTTY	Timothy Spall
NATIVE NODDY	Danny DeVito
PAY MR CLEAN-CUT	Paul McCartney
GOT SO WEIRD	Tiger Woods
I'M A TRUE BOGEY	Tobey Maguire
ME THIN MAN	Tim Henman
MEANT TO CRUNCH MICE	Martine McCutcheon
SO ANGRY OR MAD	Gordon Ramsay
I AM A SCOWLING RAT	Alistair McGowan
THAT SNAIL CHARM	Alan Titchmarsh
I AM A PLONKER – NOT SMART	Tara Palmer-Tomkinson

OSTRICHES

The ostrich, the world's largest living bird, is the only bird that provides us with leather.

An adult male bird can weigh 150 kilograms.

An ostrich's eye is the size of a tennis ball, and bigger than its brain.

An ostrich has only two toes, unlike most birds, which have three or four.

Ostriches use their powerful legs as a means of defence. They can kick a lion to death.

In Africa, ostriches are used to herd sheep.

An ostrich egg weighs the same as 24 chicken eggs.

Ostriches yawn in groups before going to sleep.

BIRD NAMES

Jackass Penguin, Wandering Albatross, Blue-footed Booby, Intermediate Egret, Short-toed Lark, Ovenbird, Solitary Sandpiper, Least Bittern, Adjutant Stork, Sacred Ibis, Horned Screamer, Turnstone, Beach Thick-knee, Laughing Gull, Fairy Tern, Masked Lovebird, Roadrunner, Screech Owl, Large Frogmouth, Turquoise-browed Motmot, Toco Toucan, Spotted Antbird, Ornate Umbrellabird, Vermilion Flycatcher, Reddish Plantcutter, Superb Lyrebird, Racquet-tailed Drongo, Magnificent Riflebird, Spotted Creeper, Striped Jungle Babbler, Fairy Bluebird, Noisy Friarbird, Bananaquit, Social Weaver, Red-legged Honeycreeper, Junglefowl, Northern Shoveller, Blue-bearded Bee-eater, Dollarbird, Buffy Fish Owl, Little Stint, Changeable Hawk Eagle, Straw-headed Bulbul, Spectacled Spiderhunter

PEOPLE WHO APPEARED IN COMMERCIALS WHEN THEY WERE CHILDREN

Jonathan Ross	Rice Krispies
Patsy Kensit	Bird's Eye frozen peas
Jodie Foster	Coppertone
Emma Bunton	Milky Bar
Leslie Ash	Fairy Liquid
Kate Winslet	Sugar Puffs
Drew Barrymore	Gainsburgers
Sarah Michelle Gellar	Burger King; she couldn't say 'burger' and so needed a speech coach
Melissa Joan Hart	Splashy, a bath toy
Reese Witherspoon	appeared in a TV commercial for a local Nashville florist when she was seven
Martine McCutcheon	Kool-Aid and Pears Soap
Lindsay Lohan	Pizza Hut, The Gap, Wendy's, Jell-O

BIRDS

During heavy snowfalls, turkeys get snow stuck in their air passages and suffocate.

Wild turkeys can fly, but farmed turkeys cannot.

The kiwi, national bird of New Zealand, is the only bird with nostrils at the end of its bill. It uses its sense of smell to find food.

The fastest bird in the world is the peregrine falcon, which can fly faster than 200 miles per hour.

The bones of a pigeon weigh less than its feathers.

Condors in the Andes of South America can live for 70 years.

Flamingos eat with their heads upside down.

Bluebirds can't see the colour blue.

Ospreys – fish-eating birds of prey – return to the same nest each year, repairing any damage caused by the weather since they last used it.

Flamingos can live for 50 years.

Pigeons can fly 600 miles in a day.

A male emperor penguin spends 60 days or more protecting his mate's eggs, which he keeps on his feet, covered with a feathered flap. During this time he doesn't eat and loses a lot of weight. After the baby birds have hatched, the female penguin returns to care for them, and the male goes away to swim, eat and rest.

Chickens, ducks and ostriches are eaten before they're born and after they're dead.

Only the male nightingale sings.

It takes about 40 minutes to hard-boil an ostrich egg.

Wild turkeys are docile, while farmed ones are aggressive.

...HMM... DID YOU JUST MOVE?

A vulture will never attack a human or animal that is moving.

The kiwi can't fly. It lives in a hole in the ground, has very poor sight and lays only one egg a year.

The albatross can sleep in flight.

A pigeon can't lay an egg unless she sees another pigeon. If another pigeon isn't available, her own reflection in a mirror will do.

Flamingos get their colour from their food. They eat tiny green algae, which turn pink during digestion.

A woodpecker can peck at the rate of 20 times a second.

Chicks breathe inside the egg. An eggshell may look solid, but it has pores that allow oxygen in and carbon dioxide out.

The grebe, a waterbird, carries its young on its back for safety. It sinks into the water until its back is level with the surface to allow the very young grebes to climb up and escape danger.

Baby robins can eat 4.25 metres of earthworms in a day.

A duck has three eyelids.

Geese often mate for life, and can pine to death at the loss of their mate.

Big Ben lost five minutes one day when a flock of starlings perched on the minute hand.

Crows have the biggest brains of any bird, relative to body size.

Chickens that lay brown eggs have red ear lobes.

The ostrich egg is 2,000 times bigger than the smallest egg, which is the hummingbird's. An ostrich egg weighs 1.2 kilograms. A hummingbird egg weighs half a gram.

To survive, many birds must eat half their own weight in food each day.

Condors can fly 10 miles without flapping their wings.

NUMBERS

Japanese researchers have calculated pi to 1.2411 trillion places. If you need to remember pi, just count the letters in each word of the sentence: 'May I have a large container of coffee?' If you are given the coffee and are polite, say: 'Thank you,' and get two more decimal places: 3.141592653 ...

The 772nd to 777th digits of pi are 999999.

For the ancient Greeks, any number more than 10,000 was a 'myriad'.

In the carol 'The Twelve Days of Christmas', the total number of gifts that 'my true love gave to me' is 364.

When 21,978 is multiplied by 4, the result is 87,912 – which is 21,978 reversed.

The Roman numerals for 1666 are MDCLXVI (1000 + 500 + 100 + 50 + 10 + 5 + 1). This is the only year featuring all the Roman numerals from the highest to the lowest.

One penny doubled every day becomes over £5 million in just 30 days.

One year is 31,557,600 seconds long.

There are 318,979,564,000 possible combinations of the first four moves in chess.

37 x 3 = 111
37 x 6 = 222
37 x 9 = 333
37 x 12 = 444
37 x 15 = 555
37 x 18 = 666
37 x 21 = 777

If you add up the numbers 1 to 100 consecutively (1 + 2 + 3 + 4 + 5, etc.) the total is 5,050.

1961 was the most recent year that could be written both upside down and the right way up and appear the same. The next year this will be possible will be 6009.

The word 'interchangeability' contains the numbers 'three', 'eight', 'nine', 'ten', 'thirteen', 'thirty', 'thirty-nine', 'eighty', 'eighty-nine', 'ninety' and 'ninety-eight'.

**Choose a number from 1 to 9.
Multiply 37,037 by the number you chose.
Multiply the result by 3.
Now you will have a number in which every digit is the same as your original number.**

The number 17 is considered unlucky in Italy.

A prime number is one that can only be divided (without leaving remainders) by itself or by one. These are all the prime numbers below 100: 2 3 5 7 11 13 17 19 23 29 31 37 41 43 47 53 59 61 67 71 73 79 83 89 97

In English, the only number that has the same number of letters as its name is FOUR. Here are some other languages and the only numbers that contain precisely the same number of letters:

Basque BEDERATZI (9)
Catalan U (1)
Czech TRI (3)
Danish and Norwegian TO (2), TRE (3), FIRE (4)
Dutch VIER (4)
Esperanto DU (2), TRI (3), KVAR (4)
Finnish VIISI (5)
German VIER (4)
Italian TRE (3)
Filipino APAT (4)
Polish PIATY (5)
Portuguese and Spanish CINCO (5)
Romanian CINCI (5)
Serbo-Croatian TRI (3)
Swedish TRE (3), FYRA (4)
Turkish DÖRT (4)

SPORTS FOR TEAMS OF 2 TO 11 PARTICIPANTS

2 – Doubles tennis

3 – Coxed pairs rowing

4 – Polo

5 – Basketball

6 – Volleyball

7 – Netball

8 – Tug-of-war

9 – Baseball

10 – Men's lacrosse

11 – Cricket and Football

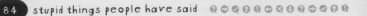

STUPID THINGS PEOPLE HAVE SAID

'Go back to Liverpool, Mr Epstein, groups with guitars are out' Dick Rowe of Decca Records, rejecting The Beatles

'Get rid of the lunatic who says he's got a machine for seeing by wireless' The editor of the *Daily Express* refusing to meet John Logie Baird – the man who invented television

'Come, come – why, they couldn't hit an elephant at this dist—' John Sedgwick, American Civil War general, just before he was shot dead

'Everything that can be invented has been invented' Charles H. Duell, Commissioner, US Office of Patents, in 1899

'This "telephone" has too many shortcomings to be seriously considered as a means of communication. The device is of no value to us' Western Union internal memo, in 1876

'Louis Pasteur's theory of germs is ridiculous fiction' Pierre Pachet, Professor of Physiology, in 1872

'Drill for oil? You mean drill into the ground to try and find oil? You're crazy' Drillers responding to Edwin L. Drake in 1859

'The wireless music box has no imaginable commercial value. Who would pay for a message sent to nobody in particular?' A businessman deciding not to invest in radio in the 1920s

'Heavier-than-air flying machines are impossible' Lord Kelvin, President of the Royal Society, in 1895

'No flying machine will ever fly from New York to Paris' Orville Wright

BEDS AND SLEEP

Zzz We spend about a third of our lives in bed.

Zzz **An adult sleeping with another adult in a standard bed has less space than a baby in a cot.**

Zzz Mark Twain wrote large parts of *Huckleberry Finn* and *The Adventures of Tom Sawyer* in bed. Robert Louis Stevenson wrote most of *Kidnapped* in bed.

Zzz **Sir Winston Churchill dictated letters and went through his red boxes in bed.**

Zzz Lots of people die in bed, but Hans Christian Andersen, the writer of fairy tales, died falling out of bed.

Zzz Sleepwalking, or somnambulism, is no joke. In 1987, an 11-year-old American boy, Michael Dixon, was found 100 miles away from his home after sleepwalking onto a train and travelling on it from Illinois to Indiana.

Zzz Insomnia is 'a chronic inability to fall asleep or to enjoy uninterrupted sleep' and it affects nearly everyone at some stage.

Zzz Famous insomniacs include Jeremy Clarkson, Colin Farrell, Justin Timberlake, David Baddiel, Winona Ryder, Robbie Williams, Gwyneth Paltrow, Daryl Hannah, Renée Zellweger, Hillary Clinton, Mariah Carey (who claims that she sleeps for just three hours a night) and Michelle Pfeiffer (who can't sleep at all some nights).

Zzz Famous people in history who were insomniacs include Abraham Lincoln, Vincent Van Gogh, Napoleon Bonaparte, Charles Dickens and Sir Winston Churchill.

THE RECORD FOR RUNNING A MILE

Roger Bannister of Great Britain was the first person to run a mile in under four minutes – in three minutes 59.4 seconds, to be exact. Other runners have since beaten his record. Here is the complete list.

TIME	NAME	PLACE	DATE
3:59.4	Roger Bannister (Great Britain)	Oxford, UK	06/05/54
3:58.0	John Landy (Australia)	Turku, Finland	21/06/54
3:57.2	Derek Ibbotson (Great Britain)	London, UK	19/07/57
3:54.5	Herb Elliott (Australia)	Dublin, Ireland	06/08/58
3:54.4	Peter Snell (New Zealand)	Wanganui, New Zealand	27/01/62
3:54.1	Peter Snell	Auckland, New Zealand	17/11/64
3:53.6	Michel Jazy (France)	Rennes, France	09/06/65

3:51.3	Jim Ryun (USA)	Berkeley, USA	17/07/66
3:51.1	Jim Ryun	Bakersfield, USA	23/07/67
3:51.0	Filbert Bayi (Tanzania)	Kingston, Jamaica	17/05/75
3:49.4	John Walker (New Zealand)	Gothenburg, Sweden	12/08/75
3:49.0	Sebastian Coe (Great Britain)	Oslo, Norway	17/07/79
3:48.8	Steve Ovett (Great Britain)	Oslo, Norway	01/07/80
3:48.53	Sebastian Coe	Zurich, Switzerland	19/08/81
3:48.40	Steve Ovett	Koblenz, Germany	25/08/81
3:47.33	Sebastian Coe	Brussels, Belgium	28/08/81
3:46.32	Steve Cram (Great Britain)	Oslo, Norway	27/07/85
3:44.39	Noureddine Morceli (Algeria)	Rieti, Italy	05/09/93
3:43.13	Hicham El Guerrouj (Morocco)	Rome, Italy	07/07/99

WAYS IN WHICH BRITAIN IS TOP OF THE WORLD

- **The longest-running show in the world – *The Mousetrap*, since 1952.**

- Highest number of botanical gardens and zoos in the world (relative to its size).

- **In Queen Victoria, the longest-reigning queen the world has ever known.**

- More public-lending libraries than any other country in the world.

- **The three most published authors of all time: William Shakespeare, Charles Dickens and Sir Walter Scott.**

- The busiest international airport in the world: London Heathrow.

- **The longest underground railway network in the world: in London.**

- Publishes more books than any other country in the world.

THINGS INVENTED IN BRITAIN

The Sandwich
The Modern Flush Toilet
The Loudspeaker
The Piggy Bank
The Lawn Mower
The Postage Stamp
The Travel Agency
The Refrigerator
The Stapler
The Electric Light
The Vending Machine
The Thermos
The Food Processor
The Hovercraft
Acrylic Paint
The CAT Scanner
Football
The Railway
Tennis
The Bicycle
Sell-by Dates
The Disposable Nappy
Airline Meals
The Underground Railway
Package Tours
Cricket

CROCODILES

If you are chased by a crocodile, run from side to side – a crocodile isn't good at making sharp turns. However, if it catches you, push your thumbs into its eyeballs – it will open its jaws and let you go at once.

Crocodiles swallow stones to help them dive deeper.

Crocodiles never outgrow the pool in which they live. If you put a baby croc in an aquarium, it would be small for the rest of its life.

A crocodile can't stick out its tongue. This is a means of self-protection. With its sharp teeth and powerful jaws it would bite off its own tongue.

The saltwater crocodile is the biggest crocodile.

A crocodile cannot move its jaws from side to side and so cannot chew. It bites off a lump of food with a snap of its jaws and then swallows it whole.

A crocodile can run at 11 miles per hour.

WHAT THEY ORIGINALLY INTENDED TO BE

Alec Baldwin	lawyer
Rowan Atkinson	electrical engineer
Eddie Izzard	accountant
Michael Palin	explorer
Dennis Quaid	musician
George Lucas	racing driver
William H. Macy	vet
Mel Gibson	chef
Angelina Jolie	funeral director
Charisma Carpenter	teacher
Tobey Maguire	chef
Dustin Hoffman	concert pianist
Lisa Kudrow	doctor
Jennifer Lopez	hairstylist
J. C. Chasez	carpenter
Lance Bass	astronaut (and passed the NASA exams)
Morgan Freeman	fighter pilot
Hannah Waterman	vet
Emma Bunton	a pony (she was a young child at the time)
Ethan Hawke	newsreader
Claudia Schiffer	lawyer
Eminem	comic-book artist
Colin Farrell	footballer

SNAKES

Rattlesnakes are born without rattles.

Most snakes lay eggs. However, the anaconda, one of the world's largest snakes, gives birth to live young, which can hunt, swim and look after themselves within a few hours of being born.

Snakes do not have eyelids, so they cannot close their eyes or blink. Instead, they have a layer of clear scales, called brille, protecting their eyes.

Rattlesnakes gather in groups to sleep through the winter. As many as 1,000 might coil up together to keep warm.

Snakes 'hear' through their jaws.

The Inland Taipan is the world's most poisonous snake. The venom it produces in one bite would be enough to kill 200,000 mice.

A snake can digest
bones and teeth
- but not fur
or hair.

When a
snake sticks
out its tongue,
it is 'smelling':
detecting chemicals
on the air.

The heads of a freak
two-headed snake
will fight over food
- despite sharing
the same stomach.

When tree snakes
fight, they try to
swallow one
another.

Some snakes can live up to a year without eating.

REPTILES

🦎 Other names for the anaconda include 'elephant-killer' (in Tamil) and 'bull-killer' (in Spanish).

🦎 **The gecko lizard can run on the ceiling because its toes have flaps of skin that provide suction.**

🦎 Tortoises are the longest-living animals. Harriet the Tortoise recently celebrated her 175th birthday in Australia. She was believed to have been picked up in the Galapagos Islands by Charles Darwin and transported to England on HMS *Beagle*, before emigrating to Australia in 1842. However, since she doesn't have a birth certificate, her age is hard to prove for certain.

🦎 **A chameleon's tongue is twice the length of its body. It uncurls its tongue to bring in food from some distance away.**

❄ The female green turtle sheds tears as she lays her eggs on the beach. This washes sand particles out of her eyes and rids her body of excess salt.

❄ **It can take the Galapagos turtle up to three weeks to digest a meal.**

❄ Marine iguanas, saltwater crocodiles, sea snakes and sea turtles are the only surviving seawater-adapted reptiles.

❄ **The flying snake of Java and Malaysia can flatten its body like a glider and sail from one tree to another.**

❄ Most lizards will replace their tail within a month of losing it.

❄ **Chameleons can move their eyes independently: one eye can look forward at the same time as the other looks back.**

❄ A python can swallow a pig whole.

WORDS

Dr Seuss invented the word 'nerd' for his book *If I Ran the Zoo*.

The word 'queueing' is the only English word with five consecutive vowels.

The word 'set' has the highest number of separate definitions in the *Oxford English Dictionary*.

Only three words in the English language end in 'dous': TREMENDOUS, HORRENDOUS, HAZARDOUS.

The word 'bigwig', meaning someone important, comes from King Louis IV of France, who used to wear big wigs.

'Almost' is the longest word in the English language with all the letters in alphabetical order.

The word 'taxi' is spelled the same way in English, French, German, Swedish, Spanish, Danish, Norwegian, Dutch, Czech and Portugucsc.

One-hundredth of a second is called a 'jiffy'.

Salma Hayek, Keira Knightley, Ozzy Osbourne, Jamie Oliver, Sir Steve Redgrave, Princess Beatrice, Tom Cruise, Whoopi Goldberg, Sir Richard Branson, Noel Gallagher, Guy Ritchie, Liv Tyler and Robbie Williams have all suffered from dyslexia.

A cat's whiskers are called 'vibrissae'.

10 body parts are only three letters long: eye, hip, arm, leg, ear, toe, jaw, rib, lip, gum.

The shortest sentence in the English language is 'Go!'

SWIMS is the longest word with 180-degree rotational symmetry – which means that it reads the same way upside down.

The phrase 'sleep tight' originated when ropes around a wooden frame were used to support a mattress. Sagging ropes could be tightened with a bed key.

'Cerumen' is the technical term for earwax.

EWE and YOU are pronounced exactly the same, yet they have no letters in common.

The suffix '-ology' means the study of something. The shortest 'ology' is 'oology' – the study of eggs.

The act of stretching and yawning is 'pandiculation'.

The first letters of the months July to November spell the name 'Jason'.

There is no single word for the back of the knee.

The names for the numbers 'eleven' and 'twelve' in English come from the Anglo-Saxon for 'one left' (*aend-lefene*) and 'two left' (*twa-lefene*). They represented going back to your left hand and starting again after reaching ten counting on your fingers.

The S-shaped opening in a violin is called the 'f-hole'.

Scribbled handwriting is known as 'griffonage'.

The oldest word in the English language is 'town'.

It is quicker to say 'world wide web', which has three spoken syllables, than it is to say its short form: 'www', which has nine syllables. (Say it out loud and see!)

THE BRAIN

The brain weighs only 1.5 kilograms but uses 20 per cent of the body's blood and oxygen.

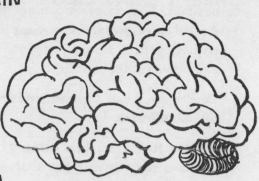

The human brain has about 100 billion nerve cells. Nerve impulses travel to and from the brain at about 170 miles per hour.

When you stub your toe, your brain registers the pain in 1/50th of a second.

If you took out your brain and unfolded it, it would cover an ironing board.

The Neanderthal's brain was bigger than yours is.

Your brain keeps growing until you are about 18.

Your skin weighs twice as much as your brain.

CREEPY CRAWLIES

* A snail can crawl across a razor blade without getting injured because it excretes a protective slime.

* **Cockroaches can survive underwater for 15 minutes.**

* Relative to its size, the ordinary house spider is eight times faster than an Olympic sprinter.

* **Slugs have four noses.**

* Earthworms have five hearts.

* **A typical bed houses over six billion dust mites.**

* If a cockroach breaks a leg, it can grow another one.

* **A spider's web is a natural clotting agent. If applied to a cut, it helps stop the flow of blood.**

* The world's termites outweigh the world's humans by 10 to one.

* **Stag beetles have stronger mandibles than humans (relative to size).**

A snail has about 25,000 teeth.

Adult earwigs can float in water for up to 24 hours.

More people are killed each year by bees than by snakes.

Australian termites have been known to build mounds six metres high and at least 30 metres wide.

The average garden snail has a top speed of 0.03 miles per hour.

Ants can't chew their food.

Mexican jumping beans jump because of a moth larva inside the bean.

The creature with the largest brain (relative to its body) is the ant.

The sensors on the feet of a red admiral butterfly are 200 times more sensitive to sugar than the human tongue.

A snail's reproductive organs are in its head.

PLANTS

- Millions of trees are planted by squirrels that bury nuts and then forget where they left them.

- **The smallest trees in the world are Greenland dwarf willows.**

- The world's largest flowering plant is 70 million times bigger than the smallest.

- **Almonds are the most widely grown and used nuts in the world.**

- Cucumbers, pumpkins and tomatoes are all fruit.

- **The canopy of a rainforest is so thick that only about one per cent of sunlight reaches the ground.**

- The giant water lily grows almost 12 centimetres a day.

- **Some bamboo plants grow a metre a day.**

- Oak trees do not produce acorns until they are at least 50 years old.

🌱 Plants grow more quickly if given warm water instead of cold.

🌱 **The cashew is a member of the poison ivy family.**

🌱 Strawberries are a member of the rose family.

🌱 **Wheat is the world's most widely cultivated plant. It is grown on every continent except Antarctica.**

🌱 Bananas contain about 75 per cent water.

🌱 **A cucumber is 96 per cent water.**

🌱 A notch in a tree will remain the same distance from the ground as the tree grows.

🌱 **Almonds are part of the peach family.**

🌱 You can figure out which way is south if you are near a tree stump. The growth rings are wider on the south side.

🌱 **1.25 million orchid seeds weigh one gram.**

🌱 A ripe cranberry bounces.

🌱 **The banana and the bird-of-paradise flower are part of the same family.**

WALT DISNEY

Born on 5 December 1901, Walt(er) Elias Disney started drawing cartoons in exchange for haircuts.

When he was 16, Disney tried to enlist in the US Army but was refused because he was too young. Eventually, he went to France as a Red Cross ambulance driver.

Disney's 1940 film *Pinocchio* is regarded as a classic, but Paolo Lorenzini, the nephew of the original author of *Pinocchio*, Carlo Lorenzini, wanted the Italian government to sue Disney for making Pinocchio too American.

When Disney set out to make his film of *Peter Pan*, he couldn't decide how to depict Tinker Bell. In the end, he decided to model her on Marilyn Monroe.

Before and after working as an ambulance driver, he worked for the postal service in Chicago and Kansas City.

In 1923, he went to Hollywood to go into partnership with his brother Roy, taking all his worldly possessions: one jacket, one pair of trousers, one shirt, two sets of underwear and a few drawing materials.

The same year, Disney took inspiration from the mice that used to play in his studio and created Mickey Mouse. He originally called him 'Mortimer', but his wife thought 'Mickey' sounded better.

For four years, Disney and his wife, the actress Lillian Bounds, lived in poverty until he had a small success with Oswald the Lucky Rabbit.

By the time of his death on 15 December 1966 at the age of 65, Disney had won more Oscars (32) than anyone else in history.

APRIL FOOLS' DAY

Probably the most famous British April Fools' Day prank was the Spaghetti Harvest on BBC TV's *Panorama* in 1957. Its presenter was the highly respected Richard Dimbleby, and millions of people were taken in when he told them about the spaghetti harvest and showed them the spaghetti 'growing' and being 'dried' in the sun.

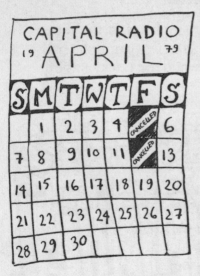

In 1979, London's Capital Radio announced that because of all the changing between British Summertime and Greenwich Mean Time, we had gained an extra 48 hours, and would have to cancel 5 April and 12 April to make up. Readers phoned in wondering what would happen to birthdays, anniversaries and other such things.

In 1976, Patrick Moore told radio listeners that while Pluto passed behind Jupiter there would be a decrease in gravitational pull. He said that if people were to jump in the air, they would feel as though they were floating. Several people rang up to say that they had done that and enjoyed the feeling.

In 1994, Mars took out full-page advertisements in newspapers announcing their 'New Biggest-ever Mars Bar'. The 'Emperor'-sized Mars Bar was 32 pounds (14 kilograms) of 'thick chocolate, glucose and milk'. It was 'on sale' for only one day: April 1.

In 1980, the BBC World Service told its listeners that Big Ben's clock-face would be replaced by a digital face.

In 1992, a joker fitted a huge sign onto the roof of the stand at the Hollywood Park racetrack reading 'Welcome to Chicago'. This was visible to passengers on flights coming into Los Angeles and caused a great deal of alarm.

PURE TRIVIA

A 'pen knife' was originally used to trim the tip of a quill.

The screwdriver was invented before the screw.

The metre was originally defined as one 10-millionth of the distance from the equator to the pole.

A fully loaded supertanker travelling at normal speed takes at least 20 minutes to stop.

Ralph and Carolyn Cummins had five children between 1952 and 1966, all of whom were born on 20 February.

Blackbird, chief of the Omaha Indians, was buried sitting on his favourite horse.

Dirty snow melts quicker than clean snow.

The most common name in Italy is Mario Rossi.

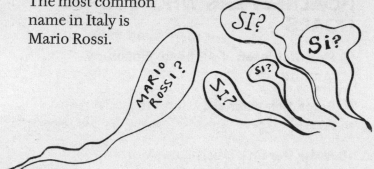

Genghis Khan's original name was Temujin. He started out as a goatherd.

No piece of paper can be folded in half more than seven times.

Whenever Beethoven sat down to write music, he poured ice water over his head.

Mickey Mouse's ears are always turned to the front, no matter which direction his nose is pointing.

On 29 March 1848, Niagara Falls stopped flowing for 30 hours because of an ice jam blocking the Niagara river.

Quackmore Duck is the name of Donald Duck's father.

GOALKEEPERS WHO SCORED GOALS

⚽ **Paul Robinson** (Tottenham Hotspur v. Watford 2007)

⚽ **Peter Schmeichel** (Aston Villa v. Everton 2001)

⚽ **Andy Goram** (Hibernian v. Morton 1988)

⚽ **Steve Ogrizovic** (Coventry City v. Sheffield Wednesday 1986)

⚽ **Steve Sherwood** (Watford v. Coventry City 1984)

⚽ **Ray Cashley** (Bristol City v. Hull City 1973)

⚽ **Peter Shilton** (Leicester City v. Southampton 1967)

⚽ **Pat Jennings** (Tottenham Hotspur v. Manchester United 1967)

THE SIMPSONS

The characters of Homer, Marge, Lisa and Maggie were given the same first names as *The Simpsons* creator Matt Groening's real-life father, mother and two sisters.

On *The Simpsons* Monopoly board, Tyre Yard is the equivalent of Old Kent Road, and Burns Manor is the equivalent of Mayfair.

Matt Groening incorporated his initials into the drawing of Homer: there's an M in his hair and his ear is the letter G.

WILD PLANT NAMES

Baldmoney,
Bloody Crane's-Bill,
Butcher's Broom, Creeping
Jenny, Devil's Bit Scabious, Devil's
Snuffbox, Dog's-Tooth-Grass, Elephant's
Ears, Enchanter's Nightshade, Fairy Foxglove,
Fat-Hen, Fool's Parsley, Gill-over-the-Ground,
Good-King-Henry, Hairy Violet, Hemlock Water-
Dropwort, Hogweed, Hound's Tongue, Jack-by-the-
Hedge, Jack-Go-to-Bed-at-Noon, Jacob's Ladder,
Lady's Bedstraw, Lady's Tresses, Lamb's Ear, Leopard's
Bane, Lords-and-Ladies, Love-in-a-Mist, Love-in-
Idleness, Mind-Your-Own-Business, Morning
Glory, None So Pretty, Old Man's Beard, Purple
Loosestrife, Red-Hot Poker, Scarlet Pimpernel,
Shepherd's Purse, Solomon's Seal, Stinking
Hellebore, Traveller's Joy, Twiggy Spurge,
Venus's Looking Glass, Viper's
Bugloss, Wavy-Hair Grass,
Witches' Butter

BEN & JERRY'S TOP 10 FLAVOURS

Cherry Garcia Ice Cream

Chocolate Chip Cookie Dough Ice Cream

Chunky Monkey Ice Cream

Chocolate Fudge Brownie Ice Cream

Half Baked Ice Cream

New York Super Fudge Chunk Ice Cream

Phish Food Ice Cream

Cherry Garcia Low Fat Frozen Yogurt

Coffee Health Bar Crunch Ice Cream

Peanut Butter Cup Ice Cream

Ben and Jerry's send their waste to local pig farmers to use as feed. Pigs love all the flavours except Mint Oreo.

THE HOUSE OF COMMONS

- MPs can wave their order papers and shout 'hear hear' to signal approval of a speech but they're not allowed to clap.

- **Electronic voting equipment is not used. MPs must walk through the 'Aye' and 'No' lobbies to vote.**

- If an MP wants to empty the public galleries he only has to say, 'I spy strangers.'

- **MPs must not mention other MPs by name. Instead, they must refer to them by their constituencies (e.g. 'The member for . . .').**

☙ When Black Rod comes to the House of Commons (for the state opening of Parliament), he is traditionally refused admission. This dates back to King Charles I and his attempts to curb the power of Parliament.

☙ There are yeomen dressed in Tudor uniform who search the cellars of the House of Commons for gunpowder.

☙ The Serjeant-at-Arms, whose office dates back to King Richard II, wears a cocked hat, cutaway coat, knee breeches, a lace ruff, black stockings and silver buckled shoes.

MARINE MAMMALS

To keep from being separated while sleeping, sea otters tie themselves together with kelp.

A baby grey whale drinks enough milk to fill more than 2,000 baby bottles a day.

Whales increase their weight 30,000,000,000 times in their first two years.

A blue whale's tongue weighs more than an elephant.

The heart of a blue whale is the size of a small car.

Next to man, the porpoise is the most intelligent creature on Earth.

The baby blue whale gains four to five kilograms in weight per hour.

Whale songs rhyme.

Whales sometimes rub up against the hulls of passing ships to get rid of parasites on their skin.

A large whale needs more than two tons of food a day.

At 188 decibels, the whistle of the blue whale is the loudest sound produced by any animal.

The blue whale weighs approximately as much as 224,000 copies of *Moby Dick*.

Sea otters have the densest fur of any creature – 100,000 hairs per square centimetre. That's about the same in a square centimetre as a human has on his or her entire head.

A blue whale's heart beats nine times a minute.

Whales can't swim backwards.

The brain of a sperm whale weighs 7.8 kilograms, but that is only 0.02 per cent of its body weight.

Because its eyeball is fixed, the whale must move its huge body to shift its line of sight.

Dolphins can hear more than 14 times better than humans.

A dolphin's hearing is so acute that it can pick up an underwater sound from 15 miles away.

Seals sleep in snatches of one and a half minutes.

The Weddell seal can travel underwater for seven miles without surfacing for air.

A male sea lion can go for three months without eating.

ANIMAL HYBRIDS

Mule: cross between a male donkey and a female horse

Hinny: cross between a male horse and a female donkey

Zeedonk: cross between a zebra and a donkey

Wolfdog: cross between a wolf and a dog

Liger: cross between a male lion and a female tiger

Tigon: cross between a male tiger and a female lion

Cama: cross between a camel and a llama

Wolphin: cross between a whale and a dolphin

LEAP YEARS

February 29 occurs once every four years because instead of precisely 365 days in a year there are 365 and a quarter. (It takes the Earth 365 and a quarter days to go around the Sun and complete an astronomical year.) The extra day every four years allows the man-made calendar to catch up with the astronomical calendar.

In years made up of 365 days, the date that is a Monday in one year will be a Tuesday in the next and a Wednesday in the third, but when the fourth year comes along with its extra day, it will 'leap' over the Thursday to fall instead on the Friday.

On Leap Year's Day in 1984, Lisa Dluchik of Swindon was born. Her mother Suzanne was also born on Leap Year Day (1956). The odds against a mother and a daughter both being born on February 29 are two million to one.

WONDERFULLY NAMED CHARLES DICKENS CHARACTERS

Doctor Neeshawts	*The Mudfog Papers*
Oswald Pardiggle	*Bleak House*
Paul Sweedlepipe	*Martin Chuzzlewit*
Doctor Soemup	*The Mudfog Papers*
Mortimer Knag	*Nicholas Nickleby*
Augustus Moddle	*Martin Chuzzlewit*
Quebec Bagnet	*Bleak House*
Simon Tappertit	*Barnaby Rudge*
Mercy Pecksniff	*Martin Chuzzlewit*
Morleena Kenwigs	*Nicholas Nickleby*
Chevy Slyme	*Martin Chuzzlewit*
Dick Swiveller	*The Old Curiosity Shop*
Conkey Chickweed	*Oliver Twist*
Sophy Wackles	*The Old Curiosity Shop*
Minnie Meagles	*Little Dorrit*
Canon Crisparkle	*The Mystery of Edwin Drood*
Peepy Jellyby	*Bleak House*
Nicodemus Boffin	*Our Mutual Friend*
Count Smorltork	*The Pickwick Papers*

CHARLES DICKENS

Dickens's father was a navy pay clerk who was made redundant and ended up in debtors' prison. Young Charles worked in a blacking factory to help the family's finances.

Dickens used his father as the inspiration for Mr Micawber, the ever-optimistic character from *David Copperfield*.

Later, Dickens became a journalist – working first as a court reporter and eventually graduating to editor.

Dickens had fainting fits. He gave dramatic readings of his books and sometimes worked himself up into such a state of excitement that he keeled over.

Dickens was an insomniac. He always made sure his bed pointed due north and that he was positioned in the absolute centre of it.

In his letters to his wife, Kate, Dickens called her his 'dearest mouse' and his 'darling pig'.

ALL THE KINGS & QUEENS OF ENGLAND AND THE UNITED KINGDOM SINCE 1066:

House of Normandy

1066–1087 William I
1087–1100 William II
1100–1135 Henry I
1135–1154 Stephen

House of Plantagenet

1154–1189 Henry II
1189–1199 Richard I
1199–1216 John
1216–1272 Henry III
1272–1307 Edward I
1307–1327 Edward II
1327–1377 Edward III
1377–1399 Richard II

House of Lancaster

1399–1413 Henry IV
1413–1422 Henry V
1422–1461 Henry VI

House of York

1461–1483 Edward IV
1483 Edward V
1483–1485 Richard III

House of Tudor

1485–1509 Henry VII
1509–1547 Henry VIII
1547–1553 Edward VI
1553–1558 Mary I
1558–1603 Elizabeth I

House of Stuart

1603–1625 James I
1625–1649 Charles I
1649–1653 Commonwealth/ protectorate
1653–1658 Protectorate of Oliver Cromwell
1658–1659 Protectorate of Richard Cromwell

House of Stuart restored

1660–1685 Charles II
1685–1688 James II
1689–1694 William
and Mary (jointly)

House of Orange

1694–1702 William III
(sole ruler)
1702–1714 Anne

House of Hanover

1714–1727 George I
1727–1760 George II
1760–1820 George III
1820–1830 George IV
1830–1837 William IV
1837–1901 Victoria

House of Saxe-Coburg

1901–1910 Edward VII

House of Windsor

1910–1936 George V
(a Saxe-Coburg
until 1917)
1936 Edward VIII
1936–1952 George VI
1952– Elizabeth II

THE LONGEST-SERVING BRITISH MONARCHS SINCE 1066

KING/QUEEN	No. OF YEARS	DATE
Queen Victoria	64	1837–1901
King George III	60	1760–1820
Queen Elizabeth II	56	1952–
King Henry III	56	1216–1272
King Edward III	50	1327–1377
Queen Elizabeth I	45	1558–1603
King Henry VI	39	1422–1461
King Henry VIII	38	1509–1547
King Henry I	35	1100–1135
King Henry II	35	1154–1189
King Edward I	35	1272–1307

HERE'S A RHYME TO HELP YOU REMEMBER ALL THE MONARCHS FROM 1066 TO THE PRESENT DAY

Willie, Willie, Harry, Ste,
Harry, Dick, John, Harry three,
One two three Edward, Richard Two,
Henry, four, five, six, then who?
Edward four, five, Dick the Bad,
Harry twain then Ned the lad,
Mary, Bessie, James the vain,
Charlie, Charlie, James again,
William and Mary, Ann Gloria,
Four Georges, William, then Victoria,
Edward, George, then Ned the eighth
quickly goes and abdicateth,
Leaving George, then Liz the second,
And with Charlie next it's reckoned
That's the way our monarchs lie
Since Harold got it in the eye!

SMILES

'A smile is a curve that sets everything straight' Phyllis Diller

'Peace begins with a smile' Mother Teresa

'My best feature's my smile. And smiles - pray heaven - don't get fat' Jack Nicholson

'Start every day off with a smile and get it over with' W. C. Fields

'I have witnessed the softening of the hardest of hearts by a simple smile' Goldie Hawn

'Smile, it is the key that fits the lock of everybody's heart' Anthony J. D'Angelo

'Before you put on a frown, make absolutely sure there are no smiles available' Jim Beggs

'It is almost impossible to smile on the outside without feeling better on the inside' Anon.

'What sunshine is to flowers, smiles are to humanity' Joseph Addison

'Smile, for everyone lacks self-confidence and more than any other one thing a smile reassures them' André Maurois

'If you smile when no one else is around, you really mean it' Andy Rooney

'Beauty is power; a smile is its sword' John Ray

'A smile is an inexpensive way to change your looks' Charles Gordy

BATS

- There are giant bats in Indonesia with a wingspan of nearly 1.8 metres.

- **The common little brown bat of North America is, for its size, the world's longest-lived mammal. It can live to the age of 32.**

- There is a bat that lives on scorpions and is immune to their stings.

Frog-eating bats find and identify edible frogs by listening to the mating calls. Frogs counter this by hiding and using short calls that are hard to locate.

Fishing bats use echolocation so well they can detect a hair's breadth of minnow fin above a pond surface.

Vampire bats adopt orphans, and have been known to risk their lives to share food with less fortunate roost-mates.

Of all the mammal species in the world, almost a quarter are bats.

Bats turn left when leaving a cave.

African heart-nosed bats can hear the footsteps of a beetle on sand two metres away.

The world's smallest mammal (where skull size is the defining factor) is the bumblebee bat of Thailand.

THE NAMES FAMOUS PEOPLE GAVE TO THEIR PETS

PERSON	PET	NAME
Reese Witherspoon	Dog: Bulldog	Frank Sinatra
Mariah Carey	Dogs: Shih-tzus Jack Russell Yorkshire Terrier	Bing and Bong Jack Ginger
Johnny Vaughan	Dog: British Bulldog	Harvey
Michael Stipe	Dog: Terrier	Helix
Wayne Rooney	Dog: Chow-Chow	Fizz
Britney Spears	Dogs: Yorkshire Terriers Rottweiler Poodle	Mitzy and Baby Cane Lady
Natalie Imbruglia	Dog: King Charles Spaniel	Charlie

Ozzy Osbourne	Dog: Bulldog	Baldrick
Samantha Mumba	Dog: Shih-tzu	Foxy
Sarah Michelle Gellar	Dog: Maltese Terrier	Thor
Drew Barrymore	Dog	Flossie
Melissa Joan Hart	Duck	Flipper
Kirsten Dunst	Cats	Inky, Taz and Zorro
Hilary Swank	Rabbit Parrot Cat	Luna Seuss Deuce
Leonardo DiCaprio	Dog: Poodle	Rufus
Jim Carrey	Dog: Labrador	Hazel
Robbie Williams	Cat	Our Lady Kid
Geri Halliwell	Dog: Shih-tzu	Harry

RABBITS

Rabbits are the fifth most popular pet in Britain (after goldfish, tropical fish, cats and dogs).

Rabbits are sociable creatures that live in large groups in underground burrows or warrens. The most popular names for British (pet) rabbits are – in order – Thumper, Flopsy and Charlie.

Rabbits can see behind themselves without turning their head.

Rabbits twitch their noses constantly because they depend on their sense of smell to warn them of danger.

The Ryukyu rabbit and Mexico's volcano rabbit are among the rarest mammals in the world.

The highest a rabbit has ever jumped is 1.5 metres.

A farmer introduced 24 wild rabbits into Australia in 1859. There are now an estimated 300 million rabbits there.

Famous rabbits include: Brer Rabbit, the White Rabbit (in *Alice's Adventures in Wonderland*), Hazel, Fiver, Bigwig, etc. (in *Watership Down*), Peter Rabbit, Benjamin Bunny, Bucky O'Hare, Rabbit (in A. A. Milne's *Winnie-the-Pooh* stories), Peter Cottontail, Bugs Bunny, Harvey (James Stewart's imaginary best friend in the 1950 film *Harvey*), Lola (in the film *Space Jam*), the Monster of Caer Bannog (in the film *Monty Python and the Holy Grail*), Oswald the Lucky Rabbit, Roger Rabbit, Thumper (in the film *Bambi*), Babs Bunny (in Steven Spielberg's *Tiny Toon Adventures*), Bean Bunny (in *The Muppets*), Benny Rabbit (in *Sesame Street*), the freaky rabbit in *Donnie Darko*, the Easter Bunny.

BIZARRE PLACE NAMES

Agenda	Wisconsin, USA
Asbestos	Canada
Banana	Australia
Belcher	Louisiana, USA
Bird-in-Hand	Pennsylvania, USA
Blubberhouses	Yorkshire
Boom	Belgium
Boring	Oregon, USA
Chicken	Alaska, USA
Chunky	Mississippi, USA
Ding Dong	Texas, USA
Drain	Oregon, USA
Eye	Suffolk
Hell	Norway
How	Wisconsin, USA
Humpty Doo	Australia
Lower Slaughter	Gloucestershire
Loyal	Oklahoma, USA
Luck	Wisconsin, USA
Mars	Pennsylvania, USA
Matching Tye	Essex
Medicine Hat	Canada
Moron	Mongolia

Nasty	Hertfordshire
Natters	Austria
Normal	Illinois, USA
Parachute	Colorado, USA
Peculiar	Missouri, USA
Pity Me	County Durham
Puzzletown	Pennsylvania, USA
Rottenegg	Austria
Rough and Ready	California, USA
Secretary	Maryland, USA
Silly	Belgium
Simmering	Austria
Siren	Wisconsin, USA
Snapfinger	Georgia, USA
Spit Junction	Australia
Surprise	Arizona, USA
Tiddleywink	Wiltshire
Tightwad	Missouri, USA
Toast	North Carolina, USA
Truth or Consequences	New Mexico, USA
Useless Loop	Australia
Vulcan	Canada
Wham	Yorkshire
Zig Zag	Australia

DAFT LABELS

On a packet of Sainsbury's peanuts: 'Warning: Contains nuts.'

On a hairdryer: 'Do not use while sleeping.'

On a bar of Dial soap: 'Directions: Use like regular soap.'

On Tesco's tiramisu dessert (printed on bottom of box): 'Do not turn upside down.'

On Marks & Spencer bread pudding: 'Product will be hot after heating.'

On packaging for a Rowenta iron: 'Do not iron clothes on body.'

On Boots children's cough medicine: 'Do not drive a car or operate machinery after taking this medication.'

On Nytol Sleep Aid: 'Warning: May cause drowsiness.'

On a set of Christmas lights: 'For indoor or outdoor use only.'

On a Japanese food processor: 'Not to be used for the other use.'

On a child's Superman costume: 'Wearing of this garment does not enable you to fly.'

On a Swedish chainsaw: 'Do not attempt to stop chain with your hands.'

On a bottle of Palmolive dishwashing liquid: 'Do not use on food.'

HOW VALUES IN A GAME OF MONOPOLY COMPARE TO REAL LIFE

'DRUNK IN CHARGE' FINE £20

Someone found drunk in charge of a vehicle could expect a fine in the region of £500 – as well as a year's disqualification.

MAKE GENERAL REPAIRS ON ALL OF YOUR HOUSES. FOR EACH HOUSE PAY £25; FOR EACH HOTEL PAY £100

To make general repairs on a house – and assuming three men working for a week – would cost about £1,400; to make general repairs on a hotel – and assuming twelve men working for four weeks – would cost about £20,000.

PAY SCHOOL FEES OF £150

Parents of a child boarding at a public school can expect to pay an average of £25,000 per year. (State schools are free.)

YOU HAVE WON SECOND PRIZE IN A BEAUTY CONTEST, COLLECT £10

The runner-up in a typical small-town beauty contest could expect to win £250.

💰 DOCTOR'S FEE £50

A Harley Street doctor will typically charge £120 for an initial consultation. (Of course, your GP doesn't charge for a consultation.)

💰 MAYFAIR

In Monopoly, a house costs £200. A four-bedroomed house in Mayfair would today cost a minimum of £4,000,000.

💰 SPEEDING FINE £15

The price of a fixed speeding ticket is now £60 + 3 penalty points.

💰 WIN A CROSSWORD COMPETITION – COLLECT £100

This is exactly how much some magazines give away in their monthly crossword competitions.

💰 PAY HOSPITAL £100

At a private hospital, a basic operation such as having tonsils removed costs about £2,000. (Of course, on the NHS it's free.)

FREE
PARKING

💰 FREE PARKING

What, in Central London?

A GUIDE TO INTERNATIONAL REGISTRATION CAR NUMBERPLATES

A — Austria
AFG — Afghanistan
AL — Albania
AND — Andorra
AUS — Australia
B — Belgium
BD — Bangladesh
BDS — Barbados
BG — Bulgaria
BOL — Bolivia
BR — Brazil
BRN — Bahrain
BRU — Brunei
BS — Bahamas
BVI — British Virgin Islands
BY — Belarus
C — Cuba
CAM — Cameroon
CDN — Canada
CH — Switzerland
CI — Ivory Coast
CL — Sri Lanka (formerly Ceylon)
CO — Colombia
CR — Costa Rica
CYF — Cyprus
CZ — Czech Republic

D — Germany
DK — Denmark
DOM — Dominican Republic
DY — Benin (formerly Dahomey)
DZ — Algeria
E — Spain
EAK — Kenya
EAT — Tanzania
EAU — Uganda
EC — Ecuador
ES — El Salvador
EST — Estonia
ET — Egypt
ETH — Ethiopia
F — France
FIN — Finland
FJI — Fiji
FL — Liechtenstein
G — Gabon
GB — United Kingdom
GBA — Alderney
GBG — Guernsey
GBJ — Jersey
GBM — Isle of Man
GBZ — Gibraltar
GCA — Guatemala

GE — Georgia
GH — Ghana
GR — Greece
GUY — Guyana
H — Hungary
HK — Hong Kong
HKJ — Jordan
HR — Croatia
I — Italy
IL — Israel
IND — India
IR — Iran
IRL — Ireland
IRQ — Iraq
IS — Iceland
J — Japan
JA — Jamaica
K — Cambodia
KWT — Kuwait
KZ — Kazakhstan
L — Luxembourg
LAO — Laos
LAR — Libya
LB — Liberia
LS — Lesotho
LT — Lithuania
LV — Latvia
M — Malta
MA — Morocco

MAL Malaysia	**RG** Guinea	**SYR** Syria
MC Monaco	**RH** Haiti	**T** Thailand
MD Moldova	**RI** Indonesia	**TCH** Chad
MEX Mexico	**RIM** Mauretania	**TG** Togo
MGL Mongolia	**RL** Lebanon	**TJ** Tajikistan
MK Macedonia	**RM** Madagascar	**TM** Turkmenistan
MOC Mozambique	**RMM** Mali	**TN** Tunisia
MS Mauritius	**RN** Niger	**TR** Turkey
MW Malawi	**RO** Romania	**TT** Trinidad & Tobago
MYA Myanmar (formerly Burma)	**ROK** South Korea	**UA** Ukraine
N Norway	**ROU** Uruguay	**UAE** United Arab Emirates
NAM Namibia	**RP** Philippines	**USA** United States of America
NAU Nauru	**RSM** San Marino	**UZ** Uzbekistan
NEP Nepal	**RU** Burundi	**VN** Vietnam
NGR Nigeria	**RUS** Russia	**WAG** Gambia
NIC Nicaragua	**RWA** Rwanda	**WAL** Sierra Leone
NL Netherlands	**S** Sweden	**WD** Dominica
NZ New Zealand	**SA** Saudi Arabia	**WG** Grenada
P Portugal	**SCG** Serbia & Montenegro	**WL** St Lucia
PA Panama	**SCN** St Kitts & Nevis	**WS** Western Samoa
PE Peru	**SD** Swaziland	**WV** St Vincent
PK Pakistan	**SGP** Singapore	**YAR** Yemen
PL Poland	**SK** Slovakia	**YV** Venezuela
PNG Papua New Guinea	**SLO** Slovenia	**Z** Zambia
PY Paraguay	**SME** Surinam	**ZA** South Africa
Q Qatar	**SN** Senegal	**ZW** Zimbabwe
RA Argentina	**SO** Somalia	
RB Botswana	**STP** São Tome & Principe	
RC Taiwan	**SUD** Sudan	
RCH Chile	**SY** Seychelles	

SWEETS – AND WHEN THEY WERE INTRODUCED

Fry's Chocolate Cream – **1866**

Toblerone – **1900**

Cadbury's Dairy Milk – **1905**

Cadbury's Bournville – **1910**

Mars Bar – **1923**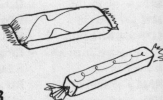

Crunchie – **1929**

Terry's All Gold – **1932**

Rowntree's Black Magic – **1933**

Kit-Kat – **1935** (although for the first two years of its existence it was known as 'Chocolate Crisp')

Aero – **1935**

Quality Street – **1936**

Dairy Box – **1936**

Rolo – **1937**

Milky Bar – **1937**

Smarties – **1937**

Cadbury's Roses – **1938**

Bounty – **1951**

Galaxy – **1958**

Picnic – **1958**

After Eight – **1962**

Toffee Crisp – **1963**

Twix – **1967**

Yorkie – **1976**

Cadbury's Eclairs – **1974** launched nationally in the UK (around non-nationally since 1960s)

Cadbury's Caramel, Double Decker, Yorkie and Lion Bar – **1976**

Drifter – **1980**

Wispa – **1983**

Boost – **1985**

Twirl – **1987**

Cadbury's White Buttons – **1989**

Timeout – **1992**

Fuse – **1996** (40 million bars sold in the first week)

Maverick – **1997**

Cadbury's Miniature Heroes, Cadbury's Giant Buttons, Kit-Kat Chunky – **1999**

Cadbury's Brunchbar, Dream, Snow Flake – **2001**

Kit-Kat Kubes – **2003**

Fruity Smarties, Kit-Kat Editions – **2004**

METEOROLOGY

Heavy rain pours down at the rate of about 20 miles per hour.

The water we drink is three billion years old.

All snow crystals are hexagonal.

On 17 July 1841, a shower of hail and rain in Derby was accompanied by a fall of hundreds of small fish and frogs – some of them still alive.

An ordinary raindrop falls at about seven miles per hour.

Small clouds that look like they have broken off from bigger clouds are called scuds.

It would take seven billion particles of fog to fill a teaspoon. A cubic mile of fog is made up of less than a gallon of water.

A snowflake can take up to an hour to land.

One centimetre of rain is equal to 10 centimetres of snow.

On 14 August 1979, a rainbow over North Wales lasted for three hours.

To see a rainbow, you must have your back to the sun.

DOGS

There are some seven million dogs in the UK. The most popular breeds are Labradors, Alsatians, West Highland white terriers and Golden Retrievers.

Three out of every 10 Dalmatians suffer from a hearing disability.

Dogs can tell non-identical twins apart by smell, but they cannot do the same with identical twins.

In 1931 Ella Wendel of New York died and left £15 million to her poodle.

A 'Seizure Alert' dog can alert its owner when he or she is about to have an epileptic seizure.

At the end of the First World War, the German government trained the first guide dogs to assist blind war veterans.

The most popular names for dogs in the UK are Sam, Trixie, Polly and Spot.

The Queen is the world's most famous owner of Corgis. The names she's given to her dogs include Fable, Myth, Shadow, Jolly and Chipper.

The breeds most likely to bite are Alsatians, Chows and Poodles.

The breeds least likely to bite are Golden Retrievers, Labradors and Old English Sheepdogs.

The most intelligent dog breeds are (in order): Border Collie, Poodle, Alsatian and Golden Retriever.

Dogs don't need to eat citrus fruit because they make their own vitamin C.

They sell toupees for dogs in Japan.

Dogs on film *Beethoven*, *The Fox and the Hound*, *101 Dalmatians*, *K-9*, *Lady and the Tramp*, *Oliver & Company*, *Turner & Hooch* (but not *Reservoir Dogs*).

Greyhounds have better eyesight than any other dog.

Paris is said to have more dogs than people.

Noseprints are the most reliable way to identify dogs.

Dogs in literature: Nana in *Peter Pan* by J. M. Barrie; Toto in *The Wizard of Oz* by L. Frank Baum; Timmy in *The Famous Five* books by Enid Blyton; Edison in *Chitty Chitty Bang Bang* by Ian Fleming; Bullseye in *Oliver Twist* by Charles Dickens; Jip in *Dr Dolittle* by Hugh Lofting; Argos in *The Odyssey* by Homer.

The world's smallest dog – the Teacup Chihuahua – weighs less than 500 grams when fully grown.

A dog can't hear the lowest key on a piano.

'A dog teaches a boy fidelity, perseverance and to turn round three times before lying down.' (Robert Benchley)

Every dog except the chow has a pink tongue – the chow's tongue is jet black.

Two dogs survived the sinking of the *Titanic*.

Greyhounds can reach their top speed of 45 miles per hour in just three strides.

The Basenji is the only dog that doesn't bark.

REAL NAMES OF FISH & CHIP SHOPS

Don't Tell a Sole	Margate
Fryer Tux Plaice	Ramsbottom
The Battersea Cod's Home	Battersea
The Wye Fry	Lydbrook, Gloucs
Vinegar Jones	Bowness
The Contented Sole	Hoyland Common, near Barnsley
The Fat Friar	Batheaston, Bath
The Starchip Enterprise	Weston
Flash in the Pan	County Antrim
The Cod Father	Billericay
The Little Chip	Gateshead
Mr Chips	Inverness
Codswallop	Frome
The Frying Squad	Bournemouth
Our Plaice	Broadstairs
Rock & Sole	Richmond
Cutty Shark	Durham

POTATOES

Sir Walter Raleigh introduced potatoes to Europe in the late 16th century and grew them at his Irish estate near Cork.

When the potato was introduced here, religious leaders denounced it because it wasn't mentioned in the Bible.

Potatoes are grown worldwide in over 125 countries (even in space - in 1995). China is the world's largest producer.

The Quechua Indians of South America have more than 1,000 different names for potatoes.

Potatoes are the world's fourth food staple - after wheat, corn and rice.

Every year enough potatoes are grown worldwide to cover a four-lane motorway circling the world six times.

The potato is about 80 per cent water and 20 per cent solids and is related to the tomato and tobacco.

King Louis XVI of France wore potato blossoms in his buttonhole while Marie Antoinette wore them in her hair.

Some superstitious people say you should carry a potato in your pocket to ease toothache.

The word 'spud' comes from the name for a narrow flat spade that was used for digging up potatoes.

Britons eat an average of 110 kilograms of potatoes every year – not quite as much as the Germans.

The Incas measured time by how long it took for potatoes to cook.

The botanical name for the common potato is *Solanum tuberosum*.

If you unscrew a light bulb and the bulb breaks, cut a potato in half and push the potato in the socket and turn. It should remove the remainder of the bulb.

Mr Potato Head was the first toy to be advertised on American television.

In 1778 Prussia and Austria fought the Potato War in which each side tried to starve the other by consuming their potato crop.

During the Alaskan Klondike gold rush of the 1890s, potatoes were so valued for their vitamin C content that miners traded gold for them.

Potatoes were first eaten more than 6,000 years ago by natives (later Incas) living in the Andes mountains of Peru.

FLAGS

The state flag of Alaska was designed by a 13-year-old boy.

Egypt, Dominica, Mexico, Fiji, Zambia and Kiribati all have birds on their flags.

Texas is the only US state allowed to fly its state flag at the same height as the US flag.

The Dominican Republic has the only national flag with a Bible on it.

Cyprus has its outline on its flag.

Nepal is the only country without a rectangular flag.

Libya has the only flag that's one colour (green) with nothing else on it.

ECCENTRIC EVENTS

Q World Screaming Championships (**Poland**)

Q Stilton Cheese-rolling Competition (**Stilton, Cambridgeshire**)

Q World Nettle-eating Championships (**Marshwood, Dorset**)

Q Air Guitar World Championships (**Finland**)

Q World Bog-snorkelling Championships (**Llanwrtyd Wells, Wales**)

Q World Walking-the-Plank Championships (**Isle of Sheppey, Kent**)

Q World Gurning Championships (**Egremont, Cumbria**)

Q Annual World Elephant Polo Association Championships (**Kathmandu, Nepal**)

Q World's Championship Duck-calling Contest and Wings Over the Prairie Festival (**Arkansas, USA**)

- **Q** Odalengo Truffle-hunting Competition (**Italy**)

- **Q** World Pea-throwing Competition (**Lewes, East Sussex**)

- **Q** World Mosquito-killing Championship (**Finland**)

- **Q** Trie-sur-Baïse Pig-screaming Championship (**France**)

- **Q** Polar Bear Jump-off (**Alaska, USA**)

- **Q** Biggest Liar in the World Competition (**Santon Bridge, Cumbria**)

- **Q** The World Wife-carrying Championships (**Finland**)

- **Q** Burning Tar Barrels (**Ottery St Mary, Devon**)

- **Q** Australia Day Cockroach Races (**Australia**)

- **Q** Summer Redneck Games (**Georgia, USA**) – includes spitball bug zapping, hubcap hurling, watermelon-seed spitting, bobbing for pigs' feet and the mud-pit bellyflop

- **Q** World Worm-charming Championships (**Nantwich, Cheshire**)

- Q Kiruna Snowball-throwing Contest (**Sweden**)

- Q World Shovel Race Championships (**New Mexico, USA**)

- Q Penny Farthing World Championships (**Tasmania**)

- Q Great Mushroom Hunt Championships (**Illinois, USA**)

- Q Munich Festival Beer-drinking Challenge (**Germany**)

- Q Annual Bat-flight Breakfast (**New Mexico, USA**)

- Q Bognor Birdman Competition (**Bognor Regis, West Sussex**)

- Q Great Tomato Fight (**Spain**)

- Q Annual Roadkill Cook-off (**West Virginia, USA**)

- Q Scarecrow Festival (**Wray, Lancashire**)

TODAY THERE ARE ABOUT 6,700,000,000 PEOPLE ON OUR PLANET . . .

Here are the best projections for the future:

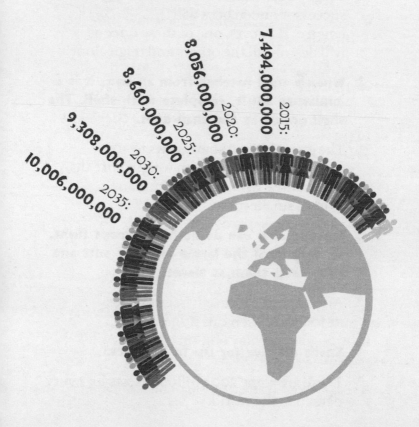

2015: 7,494,000,000

2020: 8,056,000,000

2025: 8,660,000,000

2030: 9,308,000,000

2035: 10,006,000,000

CREEPY CRAWLIES

🐞 **A bee is more likely to sting you on a windy day.**

🐞 A queen bee lays a number of eggs from which successor queen bees will emerge. However, one of these queens will destroy all the others and reign alone.

🐞 **When a snail hatches from an egg, it is a miniature adult, complete with shell. The shell grows as the snail does.**

🐞 The giant African snail grows to 30 centimetres long and can weigh more than 500 grams – which is heavier than the world's smallest dog.

🐞 **Amazon ants can do nothing except fight, so they steal the larvae of other ants and then keep them as slaves.**

🐞 After eating, a housefly regurgitates its food and then eats it again.

🐞 **Snails can live for up to 10 years.**

🐞 There are some 200 million insects for every person in the world.

When a female spider dies, she is eaten by her babies.

 Every year, insects consume 10 per cent of the world's food supply.

Centipedes always have an uneven number of pairs of legs.

Cockroaches like to eat the glue on the back of stamps.

Each of a dragonfly's eyes contains 30,000 lenses.

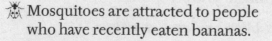

The Madagascan hissing cockroach gives birth to live young (rather than laying eggs) – it is one of very few insects to do this.

The cockroach is the fastest thing on six legs: it can cover a metre in a second.

Mosquitoes are more attracted to the colour blue than any other colour.

Mosquitoes are attracted to people who have recently eaten bananas.

ANIMALS

No new animals have been domesticated in the last 4,000 years.

The world's biggest frog is bigger than the world's smallest antelope.

A pig sleeps on its right side.

Deer can't eat hay.

Pigs are the cleanest farm animals. They will even take a shower if one is available.

An armadillo digs so fast it can completely bury itself in less than two minutes.

Hamsters like to eat crickets.

The placement of a donkey's eyes in its head enables it to see all four feet at the same time.

The red kangaroo of Australia can leap more than eight metres in one bound.

Beaver teeth are so sharp that Native Americans once used them as knife blades.

Hamsters blink one eye at a time.

There are more than 150 breeds of horse. China has the highest horse population in the world: nearly 11 million.

Rats can swim for half a mile without resting, and they can tread water for three days.

Rats are omnivorous, which means they eat almost any kind of food, including dead and dying members of their own species.

Anteaters can stick out their tongues up to 160 times a minute.

A rat will find its way through a maze more easily if you play Mozart to it.

A rat would rather have a boiled sweet than some cheese.

An angry gorilla pokes out its tongue.

A moose doesn't have good eyesight, and will sometimes approach a car, thinking it is another moose.

Kangaroos can't walk backwards.

An iguana can stay underwater for 28 minutes.

PURE TRIVIA

A 340g jar of peanut butter contains about 548 peanuts.

Thomas Edison, the inventor of the light bulb, was afraid of the dark.

More people use blue toothbrushes than red ones.

Until 1687, clocks only had an hour hand.

You can make nine hexagonal pencils with the same amount of wood it takes to make eight round ones.

A plastic container can resist decomposition for 50,000 years.

The most abundant metal in the Earth's crust is aluminium.

There is enough lead in the average pencil to draw a line 35 miles long.

65 per cent of Elvis impersonators are of Asian descent.

The average four-year-old child asks over 400 questions a day.

The decibel was named after Alexander Graham Bell, the inventor of the telephone.

Alexander Graham Bell never phoned his wife or his mother as both were deaf.

More than half the world's people have never made or received a telephone call.

The Eiffel Tower has 2.5 million rivets, 1,792 steps and can vary in height (according to the temperature) by as much as 15 centimetres.

Bugs Bunny was originally called Happy Rabbit.

The expression 'second string', meaning replacement or back-up, comes from the Middle Ages. An archer always carried a second string in case the one on his bow broke.

The Jolly Green Giant turns 80 in 2008.

Tomato ketchup was once sold as a medicine.

Al Capone's older brother was a policeman in Nebraska.

GEOGRAPHY

- The Pacific Ocean, the biggest ocean, is three times larger than Asia, the biggest continent.

- It snowed in the Sahara desert on 18 February 1979.

- More than 75 per cent of the countries in the world are north of the equator.

- Two minor earthquakes occur every minute.

- The largest iceberg ever recorded was larger than Belgium. It was 200 miles long and 60 miles wide.

- Less than two per cent of the water on Earth is fresh.

- Canada derives its name from a Native American word meaning 'big village'.

- The oldest exposed surface on Earth is New Zealand's South Island.

- England is smaller than New England.

- As a result of snowfall, for a few weeks every year K2 is taller than Mount Everest.

- **If planet Earth were smooth, the ocean would cover the entire surface to a depth of 3,700 metres.**

- The Earth's surface area is 197,000,000 square miles.

- **The forests on Kauai in Hawaii are fertilized by dust from the deserts of China, 9,660 miles away.**

- A sizeable oak tree gives off 28,000 gallons of moisture during the growing season.

- **In May 1948, Mount Ruapehu and Mount Ngauruhoe, both in New Zealand, erupted simultaneously.**

- The Indonesian island of Sumatra has the world's largest flower: the *Rafflesia arnoldi*, which can grow to the size of an umbrella.

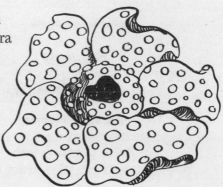

ALL THE WOMEN TO HAVE WON THE BBC'S SPORTS PERSONALITY OF THE YEAR

Zara Phillips	2006
Dame Kelly Holmes	2004
Paula Radcliffe	2002
Liz McColgan	1991
Fatima Whitbread	1987
Jayne Torvill (with Christopher Dean)	1984
Virginia Wade	1977
Mary Peters	1972
Princess Anne	1971
Ann Jones	1969
Mary Rand	1964
Dorothy Hyman	1963
Anita Lonsborough	1962

PEOPLE WHO ENTERED COMPETITIONS TO IMITATE OR IMPERSONATE THEMSELVES – AND LOST

Dolly Parton.

Charlie Chaplin.

Graham Greene, one of the greatest English writers of the 20th century, entered a competition 'to write like Graham Greene'. He came third.

Jason Donovan sent in a tape to *Stars in Their Eyes*. He was turned down.

Elvis Presley entered an Elvis lookalike contest in a US burger bar. He came third.

COMIC-BOOK SUPERHEROES AND THEIR CONCEALED IDENTITIES

Spider-Man	Peter Parker
Superman	Clark Kent
Batman	Bruce Wayne
Robin	Dick Grayson
The Green Hornet	Britt Reid
Supergirl	Linda Lee Danvers
Batgirl	Babs Gordon
The Incredible Hulk	Bruce Banner
Captain Marvel	Billy Batson
Wonder Woman	Diana Prince

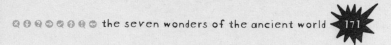

THE SEVEN WONDERS OF THE ANCIENT WORLD

1. The Pyramids of Giza (in Egypt – the only one of the seven wonders still in cxistence)

2. **The Mausoleum of Halicarnassus**

3. The Hanging Gardens of Babylon

4. **The Statue of Zeus at Olympia**

5. The Colossus of Rhodes

6. The Temple of Artemis at Ephesus

7. **The Pharos (or Lighthouse) at Alexandria**

33 THINGS TO DO BY THE AGE OF 10

(as decided by a poll of experts and celebrities recruited by the washing powder Persil for their 'dirt is good' campaign)

1. Roll down a grassy bank

2. Make a mud pie

3. Prepare a modelling-dough mixture

4. Collect frogspawn

=5. Make perfume from flower petals

=5. Grow cress on a windowsill

7. Make a papier-mâché mask

8. Build a sandcastle

9. Climb a tree

10. Make a den in the garden

11. Paint using hands and feet

12. Organize a teddy bears' picnic

13. Have a face-painting session

14. Bury a friend in the sand

15. Bake some bread

16. Make snow angels

17. Create a clay sculpture

18. Take part in a scavenger hunt

19. Camp out in the garden

20. Bake a cake

21. Feed a farm animal

22. Pick some strawberries

23. Play Pooh sticks

24. Recognize five bird species

25. Find some worms

26. Cycle through a muddy puddle

27. Make and fly a kite

28. Plant a tree

29. Build a nest from grass and twigs

30. Find 10 different leaves in the park

31. Grow vegetables

32. Make breakfast in bed for Mum and Dad

33. Create a mini assault course in the garden

SOME DEADLY AUSTRALIAN CREATURES

The blue-ringed octopus – one bite or squirt causes paralysis. Death follows in minutes.

The 'sea wasp' or box jellyfish – the survival rate from its sting is almost zero. Death follows in four minutes.

The taipan snake is 180 times more venomous than the king cobra – one bite could kill a person within three seconds.

Redback spider – the bite of the female can kill. There have been no deaths since the antivenom was found.

The funnel-web spider – one of the most dangerous spiders in the world. The bite of the male can kill a person in 15 minutes. There have been no deaths since the antivenom was found.

Textile cone shells – underwater creature with up to 12 darts, each of which has enough poison to kill someone. Death follows in minutes.

Irukandji jellyfish – this has poisonous tentacles. Swimmers, if stung, can suffer a heart attack and drown.

The saltwater crocodile – kills people because it is fast in and out of water. It can outrun a galloping horse and it kills in seconds.

The great white shark – this is the most dangerous of the many sharks in Australian waters. It kills in seconds with just one snap of its awesome teeth.

The tiger snake – death occurs within 12 hours. Antivenom is available but it must be used within 30 minutes of the bite. One snake has enough venom to kill 118 sheep.

EXTRAORDINARY BEQUESTS

In 1974, Philip Grundy, a dentist, left his dental nurse £181,000 on the condition that she didn't wear any make-up or jewellery or go out with anyone for five years.

In 1955, Juan Potomachi, an Argentinian, left more than £25,000 to his local theatre on condition that they used his skull as a prop in Shakespeare's *Hamlet*.

Mr John Bostock left £100 in his will to the manager of the local Co-op for the provision, 'until the fund be exhausted', of a bar of chocolate every week for each child under the age of five in Westgate-in-Weardale, County Durham.

In 1950, George Bernard Shaw left a large sum of money for the purpose of replacing the English alphabet of 26 letters with an alphabet of 40 letters – it was never done.

An unnamed Scotsman bequeathed each of his two daughters her weight in money. The elder, slimmer daughter received £51,200, while her younger, fatter sister got £57,433.

THE MONOPOLY SQUARES THAT ARE MOST OFTEN LANDED ON

In order:

Trafalgar Square

Go

Marylebone Station

Free Parking

Marlborough Street

Vine Street

King's Cross Station

Bow Street

Water Works

Fenchurch Street Station

Note: *The first three all have Chance and/or Community Chest cards directing you there. All properties in the top six are within a throw (or two) of jail – which can, of course, be reached via cards, the Go To Jail square or by throwing three consecutive doubles.*

FAMOUS NOVELS ORIGINALLY REJECTED BY PUBLISHERS

The Time Machine by H. G. Wells

The Mysterious Affair at Styles by Agatha Christie

Harry Potter and the Philosopher's Stone by J. K. Rowling

The Picture of Dorian Gray by Oscar Wilde

Moby Dick by Herman Melville

Northanger Abbey by Jane Austen

Catch-22 by Joseph Heller

The Wind in the Willows by Kenneth Grahame

A Time to Kill by John Grisham

The Rainbow by D. H. Lawrence

The Spy Who Came In from the Cold by John Le Carré

Animal Farm by George Orwell

Tess of the D'Urbervilles by Thomas Hardy

Lord of the Flies by William Golding

CLASSIC NOVELS AND THEIR ORIGINAL TITLES

The Time Machine (H. G. Wells):
The Chronic Argonauts

Treasure Island (Robert Louis Stevenson):
The Sea-Cook

War and Peace (Leo Tolstoy):
All's Well That Ends Well

Moby Dick (Herman Melville):
The Whale

Of Mice and Men (John Steinbeck):
Something That Happened

Gone With the Wind (Margaret Mitchell):
Ba! Ba! Black Sheep

Frankenstein (Mary Shelley):
Prometheus Unchained

and people who wrote just one novel

Anna Sewell: **Black Beauty**
Margaret Mitchell: **Gone With the Wind**
Harper Lee: **To Kill a Mockingbird**
Emily Brontë: **Wuthering Heights**
Kenneth Grahame: **The Wind in the Willows**

EXTRAORDINARY EVENTS

DOUBLE PROOF: A pair of identical American twin boys were separated at birth in 1940 and adopted by different people who didn't know each other. Each boy was named James, each boy married a woman named Linda, had a son named James Alan, and was then divorced. When they eventually met up at the age of 39, they found that their hobbies, experiences and tastes had been and were remarkably similar.

BABY LUCK: Some coincidences are just too extraordinary. In 1975 in Detroit, a baby fell out of a building 14 storeys up. Fortunately, it landed on a man named Joseph Figlock and so survived. A year later, another baby fell from the same building and survived by falling on . . . Joseph Figlock.

LET IT RAIN:
In 1986,
American
judge
Samuel
King was
annoyed
that some
jurors were
absent from
his Californian

court because of heavy rain, so he issued a decree: 'I hereby order that it cease raining by Tuesday.' California suffered a five-year drought. So in 1991 the judge decreed, 'Rain shall fall in California beginning February 27.' Later that day, California had its heaviest rainfall in a decade.

A GOLDEN SHEEP: In 1984, a Greek Orthodox priest was cooking a sheep's head when he discovered that the sheep had a jaw composed of 14-carat gold. The sheep had come from a herd owned by the priest's own brother-in-law and he couldn't come up with any explanation, nor could the Greek ministry of agriculture.

KINGS AND THEIR *UNFORTUNATE* NICKNAMES

King Rudolf the Sluggard
(King Rudolf III of Burgundy from 993 to 1032)

King Malcolm the Maiden
(King Malcolm IV of Scotland from 1153 to 1165)

King Louis the Fat
(King Louis VI of France from 1108 to 1137)

King Ferdinand the Fickle
(King Ferdinand I of Portugal from 1367 to 1383)

King Charles the Mad
(King Charles VI of France from 1380 to 1422)

King Ivan the Terrible
(King Ivan IV of Russia from 1547 to 1584)

King Louis the Stubborn
(King Louis X of France from 1314 to 1316)

King Charles the Bad
(King Charles II of Navarre from 1349 to 1387)

King Ethelred the Unready
(King Ethelred II of England from 978 to 1016)

KINGS AND THEIR *FORTUNATE* NICKNAMES

King Louis the Just
(King Louis XIII of France from 1610 to 1643)

King William the Good
(King William II of Sicily from 1166 to 1189)

King Philip the Handsome
(King Philip of Castile in 1506; he was married to Joan the Mad)

King Charles the Victorious
(King Charles VII of France from 1422 to 1461)

King Henry the Saint
(King Henry II of Germany from 1014 to 1024)

King Richard the Lionheart
(King Richard I of England from 1189 to 1199)

King Philip the Fair
(King Philip IV of France from 1285 to 1314)

King Ferdinand the Great
(King Ferdinand I of Castile from 1035 to 1065)

King Charles the Wise
(King Charles V of France from 1364 to 1380)

King Louis the Well-Beloved
(King Louis XV of France from 1715 to 1774)

REAL PEOPLE WHO'VE APPEARED IN THE *BEANO*

Chris Evans	with Dennis the Menace
Geri Halliwell	with Minnie the Minx
Linford Christie	with Billy Whizz
Ronan Keating	with Plug from the Bash Street Kids
Alan Shearer	with Ball Boy
Michael Owen	with Ball Boy
Ken Dodd	with Dennis the Menace's dog, Gnasher
Tony and Cherie Blair	with Ivy the Terrible. Tony Blair is also an honorary member of the Dennis the Menace Fan Club
Sir David Jason as Del Boy Trotter	with Roger the Dodger
Rowan Atkinson as Mr Bean	with Calamity James
Brooklyn Beckham	with Bea, Dennis the Menace's sister
Donna Air	as a 12-year-old in a photo story

PEOPLE WHO WERE BULLIED AT SCHOOL

GWYNETH PALTROW (because she was 'gawky')

HARRISON FORD (because he 'liked to hang out with girls')

ANTHEA TURNER (because of her 'posh' accent)

PRINCE CHARLES (because he was heir to the throne – was especially bullied during rugby games)

MEL GIBSON (because of his American accent at his Australian school)

SANDRA BULLOCK (because she was 'ugly')

TOM CRUISE (because he 'was always the new kid in town')

SOPHIE DAHL (by a boy who fancied her but whom she rejected)

MICHELLE PFEIFFER (because of her 'big lips')

NATALIE IMBRUGLIA ('for having big lips and big eyes')

VICTORIA BECKHAM (because of her wealthy background; girls at school would push her around and swear at her in the playground and call her names because she had spots)

WOODY ALLEN (because of his name, Allen Konigsberg – 'I'd tell them my name was Frank, but they'd still beat me up')

KATE WINSLET ('I was mentally bullied' – because of her weight)

MARTIN CLUNES (taunted about his looks)

JUDE LAW (at a comprehensive in south-east London where suspects in the Stephen Lawrence murder were pupils; he moved to a private school where he was also bullied)

DERVLA KIRWAN (because she was shy)

CHRISTINA AGUILERA (because she appeared on TV. In 2000, she got her own back on one of the bullies by driving in her sports car to the McDonald's where the girl worked. 'I heard you were working here and wanted to say hello,' she said)

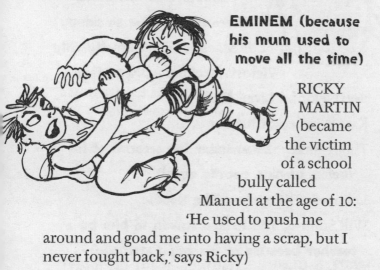

EMINEM (because his mum used to move all the time)

RICKY MARTIN (became the victim of a school bully called Manuel at the age of 10: 'He used to push me around and goad me into having a scrap, but I never fought back,' says Ricky)

FAMOUS PEOPLE AND THEIR CHILDHOOD NICKNAMES

Prince Andrew ⇨ **The Sniggerer**

Prince Edward ⇨ **Jaws**

Prince Philip ⇨ **Flop**

Liam Gallagher ⇨ **Weetabix**

Kate Moss ⇨ **Mosschops**

Michael Owen ⇨ **Mincer**

Cameron Diaz ⇨ **Skeletor**
(because she was so skinny)

Elle Macpherson ⇨ **Smelly Elly**

Victoria Beckham ⇨ **Acne Face**

Bob Geldof ⇨ **Liver Lips**

Kate Winslet ⇨ **Blubber**

Thom Yorke ⇨ **Salamander (on account of his 'weird, wonky, reptile eyes')**

Leonardo DiCaprio ⇨ **The Noodle**

Will Smith ⇨ **The Prince (given to him by a teacher because of his regal attitude)**

Johnny Depp⇨**Mr Stench**

Rachel Stevens⇨**Ratz**

Donna Air⇨**Lego Legs**

Cindy Crawford⇨**Crawdaddy**

Steven Spielberg⇨**The Retard**

Noel Gallagher⇨**Brezhnev**

Kate Hudson ⇨**Hammerhead Shark (her brother's nickname because of the space between her eyes)**

Justin Timberlake⇨**Brillo Pad (because of his curly hair)**

Robert De Niro⇨**Bobby Milk (because he was so pale)**

Nicole Kidman⇨**Stalky**

Kylie Minogue⇨**Shorty**

Davina McCall⇨**Div**

Britney Spears⇨**Boo-Boo**

Elijah Wood⇨**Little Monkey**

J. C. Chasez⇨**Mr Sleepy**

Nicole Appleton⇨**Fonzie**

Madonna⇨**Nonni (family nickname)**

FILM GAFFES

In *Charlie's Angels* (2000), when Drew Barrymore lifts up Lucy Liu to spin her around and kick the baddie, Drew calls out 'Lucy!' to get her attention – even though Lucy Liu's character's name is Alex. See also *The Doors* (1991), when Meg Ryan calls Val Kilmer Val instead of Jim, his character's name, and *The War of the Roses* (1989), in which Michael Douglas addresses Danny DeVito's character as DeVito.

In *Spider-Man* (2002), Peter shoots his web at a lamp and pulls it across the room, smashing it, but seconds later it's back on the dresser in one piece.

In *Charlie and the Chocolate Factory* (2005), when Charlie shares his Wonka bar with members of his family, he breaks his father's share into two separate bits, but when his father goes to take a bite, the two bits are still attached to one another.

In *Robin Hood: Prince of Thieves* (1991), the sheriff uses the expression '10.30'. Clocks didn't exist in the 12th century.

In *Speed* (1994), Harry (Jeff Daniels) is shot by Jack (Keanu Reeves) in the left leg but we later see him limping on the right leg.

In *Harry Potter and the Philosopher's Stone* (2001), at the start-of-term feast Harry sits down on one side of the table next to Ron. When the food is served, Harry is on the other side of the table, next to Hermione.

In *Gladiator* (2000), in a battle scene, a chariot is turned over and a gas cylinder can be seen in the back.

In *The Wedding Singer* (1998), Julia's wedding was supposed to take place on Sunday, 5 August 1985. But in 1985, 5 August was a Monday.

In *It's a Wonderful Life* (1946), the old man's cigar disappears when he sends young George to deliver a prescription.

In *The Silence of the Lambs* (1991), Clarice Starling (played by Jodie Foster) has blue eyes, but the actress playing her as a child has brown eyes.

In *The Matrix: Reloaded* (2003), there is a scene during a powercut where car headlights also go out.

PEOPLE WHO CHANGED THEIR NAMES

Sir Elton John	Reginald Dwight
Meg Ryan	Margaret Hyra
Macy Gray	Natalie McIntyre
Harry Hill	Matthew Hall
Jodie Foster	Alicia Foster
Queen Latifah	Dana Owens
Ice Cube	O'Shea Jackson
Ozzy Osbourne	John Michael Osbourne
Joaquin Phoenix	Joaquin Bottom – his surname was changed by his parents
Ms Dynamite	Niomi Daley
Demi Moore	Demetria Guynes
Sir Michael Caine	Maurice Micklewhite
Sting	Gordon Sumner
Goldie	Clifford Price
Shane Richie	Shane Roche

FAMOUS PEOPLE AND THE SPORTS THEY PLAYED

DARREN DAY was a semi-professional snooker player.

HILARY SWANK swam in the Junior Olympics; she was also a top gymnast.

QUEEN LATIFAH was a power forward on two state championship basketball teams in high school.

Sonique was a gifted pentathlete as a teenager.

GEORGE CLOONEY once tried out for the Cincinnati Reds baseball team.

HEATH LEDGER nearly became a professional ice-hockey player but chose acting over sport.

SHERYL CROW was a competitive hurdler.

RICHARD GERE won a gymnastics scholarship to the University of Massachusetts.

MATTHEW PERRY was ranked number two at tennis in Ottawa at the age of 13.

KEANU REEVES was the goalkeeper in his high school ice-hockey team, where he earned the nickname 'The Wall' and where he was voted MVP (Most Valuable Player).

ARNOLD SCHWARZENEGGER was not only a bodybuilding champion but also won the Austrian Junior Olympic Weightlifting gold medal.

TOM CRUISE was an all-round sporting star at school but he turned to acting after injuring his knee in wrestling.

IAN MCSHANE could have followed his father into a career with Manchester United but he turned down the opportunity and became an actor instead.

JENNIFER LOPEZ was a star gymnast at high school.

LIAM NEESON boxed for a local team from the age of nine until 17 (in one early match his nose was broken and he had it set on the spot by his manager).

MEL C ran for Cheshire County when she was a schoolgirl.

SARAH MICHELLE GELLAR was a competitive figure skater for three years and was ranked third in New York State.

ROLF HARRIS was Junior Backstroke Champion of all Australia in 1946.

GABBY LOGAN represented Wales at gymnastics in the 1990 Commonwealth Games.

50 CENT was a talented boxer who thought about becoming a professional.

GARY LINEKER played second XI cricket for Leicestershire and once scored a century for the MCC playing at Lord's.

PEOPLE WHO USED TO BE WAITERS/WAITRESSES

Alec Baldwin

Antonio Banderas

Jennifer Aniston

Graham Norton

Mariah Carey

Julianna Margulies

Russell Crowe

Kristin Davis

Julianne Moore

Richard Gere (once served Robert De Niro)

Dido (once dropped 16 glasses of wine and a tray on Stephen Fry when waitressing at Café Flo in London)

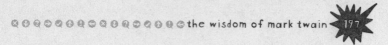

THE WISDOM OF MARK TWAIN

(the man who wrote *Tom Sawyer* and *Huckleberry Finn*)

'Courage is resistance to fear, mastery of fear, not absence of fear.'

'It is better to deserve honours and not have them than to have them and not deserve them.'

'I was born modest. Not all over but in spots.'

'Fewer things are harder to put up with than the annoyance of a good example.'

'Man is the only animal that blushes – or needs to.'

'If you tell the truth you don't have to remember anything.'

'I must have a prodigious quantity of mind. It takes me as much as a week, sometimes, to make it up.'

'Life would be infinitely happier if we could only be born at the age of eighty and gradually approach eighteen.'

'Noise proves nothing. Often a hen who has merely laid an egg cackles as if she had laid an asteroid.'

'I can live for two months on a good compliment.'

'Don't let schooling interfere with your education.'

SPORT

Some 42,000 balls are used at the Wimbledon tennis tournament each year.

When volleyball was invented in 1895, it was called mintonette.

At one stage in the 1920s, Chelsea football team had three players who were medical students.

There are two sports in which the team has to move backwards to win: tug of war and rowing. (NB Backstroke is not a team sport.)

When Len Shackleton wrote his autobiography, he included a chapter entitled 'The Average Director's Knowledge of Football'. The chapter consisted of a blank page.

A baseball hit by a bat travels as fast as 120 miles per hour – almost the same (maximum) speed as the puck in ice hockey.

There are 108 stitches on a baseball.

Australian Rules Football was originally designed to give cricketers something to play during the off-season.

PROVERBS THAT ARE CLEARLY NOT TRUE (think about them!)

An apple a day keeps the doctor away.

You can't judge a book by its cover.

Every cloud has a silver lining.

Ask no questions and you will be told no lies.

Barking dogs seldom bite.

It never rains but it pours.

PEOPLE WHO WERE EDUCATED AT HOME

Dame Agatha Christie, Gerald Durrell, C. S. Lewis, Alexander Graham Bell, the Queen, Britney Spears, Joaquin Phoenix

PEOPLE WHO WERE EXPELLED FROM SCHOOL

Nicolas Cage (from elementary school – for putting dead grasshoppers in the egg salad on picnic day)

Salma Hayek (from a Louisiana boarding school – for setting alarm clocks back three hours)

Kevin Spacey (from a military academy – for hitting a classmate with a tyre)

Jeremy Clarkson (from public school – for many minor offences which his headmaster compared to being poked in the chest every day for five years)

FAMOUS PEOPLE WHO USE THEIR MIDDLE NAMES AS FIRST NAMES

David **Jude** Law

Laura **Reese** Witherspoon

Walter **Bruce** Willis

William **Bradley** Pitt

James **Gordon** Brown

James **Paul** McCartney

PEOPLE NAMED AFTER SOMEONE/ SOMETHING FAMOUS

Halle Berry
(after the Halle Brothers department store)

Heath Ledger
(after Heathcliff in *Wuthering Heights*)

Dido
(after the African warrior queen)

Oprah Winfrey
(after Orpah, from the Bible's Book of Ruth; it was misspelt on her birth certificate)

WHAT THEY DID BEFORE BECOMING FAMOUS

J. K. Rowling – worked at the Amnesty International office in London and then at the Chamber of Commerce in Manchester

Anne Fine – teacher

Davina McCall – singing waitress in Paris

Paul O'Grady – social worker

Renée Zellweger – bartender assistant

Johnny Vaughan – grill chef, jewel courier, sales assistant, video shop manager

George Clooney – sold insurance door to door, cut tobacco in Kentucky

Russell Crowe – bingo caller

Vin Diesel – bouncer

Björk – fish-factory employee

Liam Neeson – forklift truck driver at the Guinness brewery in Dublin

Josh Hartnett – video-shop clerk

Bob Geldof – meat packer

Madonna – worked in Burger King; also as a lifeguard and a lift operator

Sir Elton John – messenger boy

Kylie Minogue – video-shop worker

Ozzy Osbourne – slaughterhouse labourer

Rod Stewart – grave digger

Vic Reeves – pig farmer

Pierce Brosnan – taxi driver

Dawn French – teacher

Angelina Jolie – embalmer

Jason Biggs – Subway sandwich maker

Ricky Gervais – pizza delivery boy

Mackenzie Crook – worked at Pizza Hut, in a chicken factory and at hospitals

Rolf Harris – postman

Keanu Reeves – managed a pasta shop in Toronto, Canada

TRAINED AS BALLET DANCERS

Morgan Freeman

Charlize Theron

Caroline Quentin

Rachel de Thame

Jane Seymour (danced with the London Festival Ballet at the age of 13)

Mira Sorvino (performed in a professional production of *The Nutcracker* at the age of 12)

Penelope Cruz

Jennifer Ellison (Under-10 World Ballet Champion, Senior Champion at 14)

Sarah Jessica Parker (was with the Cincinnati Ballet and the American Ballet Theater)

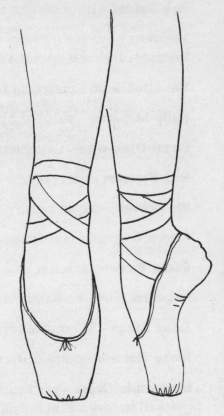

MURPHY'S LAW

The original Murphy's Law stated that:
'Anything that can go wrong will go wrong.'

Here are other applications of Murphy's Law:

> **The first place to look for something is the last place you expect to find it.**

> Whenever you make a journey by bicycle, it's always more uphill than downhill.

> **As soon as you mention something: a) if it's good, it goes away; b) if it's bad, it happens.**

> You never find something until you replace it.

> **When you call a wrong number, it's never engaged.**

In a supermarket, the other queues always move faster than yours.

The harder it is to reach an itch, the more you want to scratch it.

Friends come and go but enemies accumulate.

TOILETS AROUND THE WORLD

The Japanese have invented the Shower Toilet. It has a self-raising seat cover, a bidet, water jets, a heated seat, a hot-air dryer and a fan for the removal of smells, all operated with an infra-red control.

In 1993, Juan Bernaus was sentenced to three years' jail in Argentina for switching the 'Ladies' and 'Gents' signs round on public toilets.

An American jeweller has built the world's most expensive toilet, made of gold, diamonds, rubies and emeralds, with a mink-fur seat – it costs $175,000.

In a 1992 survey by Andrex Toilet Tissue, British public toilets were voted among the worst in the world, just ahead of those in Thailand, Greece and France.

TALKING TOILETS

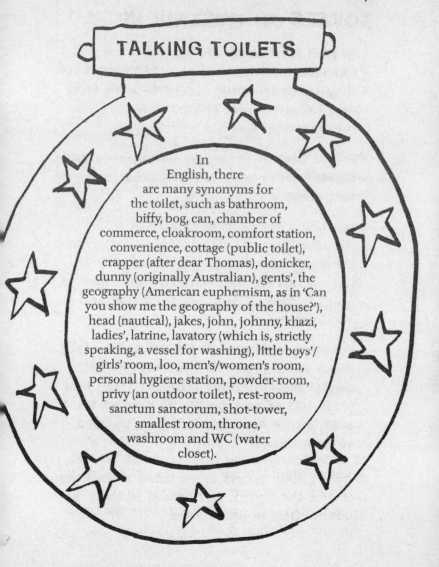

In English, there are many synonyms for the toilet, such as bathroom, biffy, bog, can, chamber of commerce, cloakroom, comfort station, convenience, cottage (public toilet), crapper (after dear Thomas), donicker, dunny (originally Australian), gents', the geography (American euphemism, as in 'Can you show me the geography of the house?'), head (nautical), jakes, john, johnny, khazi, ladies', latrine, lavatory (which is, strictly speaking, a vessel for washing), little boys'/girls' room, loo, men's/women's room, personal hygiene station, powder-room, privy (an outdoor toilet), rest-room, sanctum sanctorum, shot-tower, smallest room, throne, washroom and WC (water closet).

ROYALS ON THE THRONE

- In 1988, Australian officials built a special toilet for the Queen at a cost of £35,000. Then they decided to build a second – at the same cost – in case Prince Philip needed to go at the same time. Neither toilet was used.

- **Prince Charles insists on having his own wooden toilet seat installed wherever he's going.**

- Just before the Queen opened the Westminster and Chelsea Hospital, of which she was to be patron, officials realized that the hospital's initials would be WC – they quickly changed the name to Chelsea and Westminster.

- **Sir Winston Churchill did not believe in using toilet seats. He had them for his guests but when his plumber asked him what sort of seat he would have on his own loo, he responded, 'I have no need of such things.'**

- The death of Queen Victoria's beloved Albert was a result of poor sanitation – he died of typhoid in 1861 (in 1870, one in every 3,000 people in Britain died of typhoid).

♨ **King Edward VII bought a 'WC enclosure in the form of an attractive armchair upholstered in velvet' for the actress Lily Langtry.**

CREEPY CRAWLIES

- **A large swarm of locusts can eat 80,000 tons of corn in a day.**

- If you see a spider dismantling its web, you know a storm is on the way.

- **80 per cent of the creatures on Earth have six legs.**

- Maggots were once used to treat a bone infection called osteomyelitis.

- **There are one million ants for every person in the world.**

- The Venus flytrap takes less than half a second to slam shut on an insect.

- **Tarantulas extend and withdraw their legs by controlling the amount of blood pumped into them.**

- If you put a drop of alcohol on a scorpion, it will go mad and sting itself to death.

- **Dragonflies can fly at 30 miles per hour.**

- A species of earthworm in Australia grows to three metres long.

- **Many hairy caterpillars carry a toxin that can be painful to humans if touched.**

- From hatching to pupation, a caterpillar increases its body size 30,000 times.

- **The largest insect on Earth is the South American acteon beetle (*Megasoma acteon*), which measures 9cm by 5cm, and is 4cm thick.**

- The heaviest insect is the Goliath beetle, weighing in at 100 grams.

- **The neck of the male long-necked weevil is twice as long as its body.**

- Leeches can drink up to five times their weight in blood.

- **Insects shiver when they're cold.**

PURE TRIVIA

Half the world's population has seen at least one James Bond movie.

Malaria was originally believed to be caused by the vapour rising from swamps. The name 'malaria' means 'bad air'.

According to the ancient Chinese, swinging your arms cures headache pain.

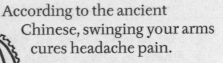

A banana-shaped stamp was once used in the country of Tonga.

Amber was once thought to be lumps of solidified sunshine.

A cat falling from the seventh floor of a building has less chance of surviving than if it falls off the twentieth floor. It takes about eight floors for the cat to realize what's going on and prepare itself.

According to Norse legend, peas were sent to Earth by the god Thor, and were only to be eaten on his day: Thursday.

The oldest known vegetable is the pea.

Aeschylus of ancient Greece is said to have died when an eagle passing overhead dropped a tortoise on his head.

The Nike 'swoosh' was designed by Caroline Davidson back in 1971. She received $35 for it.

Salvador Dalí once arrived at an art exhibition in a limousine filled with turnips.

Rabbits like licorice.

Pinocchio was made of pine.

The hundred-billionth Crayola crayon was Periwinkle Blue.

More people are killed by donkeys than in aeroplane crashes.

The colder the room you sleep in, the more likely you are to have a bad dream.

The name Wendy was made up for the book *Peter Pan*.

Donald Duck's middle name is Fauntleroy.

AROUND THE WORLD

- Disney World is bigger than the world's five smallest countries.

- **The Danish flag – dating back to the 13th century – is the world's oldest unchanged national flag.**

- There is a city called Rome on every continent.

- **Istanbul is the only city in the world to be in two continents (Europe and Asia).**

- All the continents are wider in the north than in the south.

- **The Dead Sea is really a lake.**

You could drive a car around the world **four** times with the amount of fuel in a jumbo jet.

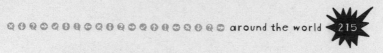

● The largest employer in the world is the Indian railway system.

● In Bhutan, all citizens officially become a year older on New Year's Day.

● The Philippine flag is displayed with its blue field at the top in times of peace and the red field at the top in times of war.

● There isn't a (real) river in the whole of Saudi Arabia.

● If all the Antarctic ice melted, the ocean level would rise nearly 75 metres, and 25 per cent of the world's land surface would be flooded.

● There are more Barbie dolls in Italy than there are Canadians in Canada.

● There are more than 15,000 different varieties of rice.

● In China, the population of over a billion shares about 200 family names.

ANIMALS

A chamois goat can balance on a pinnacle of rock no wider than a £1 coin.

All the pet hamsters in the world are descended from one female wild golden hamster found with a litter of 12 young in Syria in 1930.

It takes a sloth up to six days to digest the food it eats.

A hedgehog's heart beats 190 times a minute. This drops to 20 beats per minute during hibernation.

Cows can hear lower and higher frequencies than we can.

Porcupines can float in water.

A chimpanzee can learn to recognize itself in a mirror, but a monkey can't.

You can tell a turtle's gender by the noise it makes: males grunt, females hiss.

Cows and horses sleep standing up.

Alaska has almost twice as many caribou as people.

The underside of a horse's hoof is called a frog. The frog peels off several times a year with new growth.

A zebra is white with black stripes.

When opossums are 'playing possum', they are not really playing – they pass out from sheer terror.

Montana mountain goats can butt heads so hard that their hooves fall off.

A kangaroo can only jump when its tail is touching the ground.

Squirrels can climb faster than they can run.

The honey badger in Africa can withstand bee stings that would kill another animal.

The word rodent comes from the Latin word 'rodere', meaning to gnaw.

The ancient Egyptians trained baboons to wait at their tables.

Gorillas can't swim.

THINGS THAT NEW WORKERS ARE ASKED TO FETCH

It's a sort of initiation test because, of course, none of these things exist! Well, you try finding a tin of striped paint . . .

A tub of elbow grease, invisible nails, a pair of rubber scissors, a dozen sky-hooks, a left-handed monkey-wrench, a glass hammer, a long weight, a horizontal ladder, a right-handed mug.

GOLD

All the gold ever mined would form a heap as big as a three-bedroom house; all the gold that's still to be mined on land would only be big enough to make the garage. There is, however, much more gold in the world's oceans.

Gold is the only metal that doesn't rust – even if it's buried in the ground for thousands of years.

Pure gold is so soft that it can be moulded with the hands, which is why copper is added to it for jewellery.

India is the world's largest consumer of gold.

South Africa produces two-thirds of the world's gold.

There are just six grams of gold in an Olympic gold medal.

In the original story of Cinderella, her slippers were made of gold, not glass. And her stepsisters were beautiful on the outside – their ugliness lay within.

ELEPHANTS

Elephants sleep for about two hours per day.

Elephants walk on tiptoe – the back of the foot is made up of fat and no bone.

The brain of an African elephant weighs 7.5 kilograms – which is 0.15 per cent of the animal's total body weight. The brain of an adult human weighs 1.3–1.4 kilograms, which is about two per cent of total body weight.

Both male and female African elephants have tusks, but only male Indian elephants do.

An African elephant eats more than 200 kilograms of twigs, leaves, grass and fruit a day.

Elephants are covered with hair. You cannot see it from a distance, but at close range it is possible to see the thin coat of light hairs that covers the animal's body.

An elephant's trunk can hold nine litres of water.

Elephants are not afraid of mice.

An elephant's trunk has 40,000 muscles but no bone.

At birth an Indian elephant weighs around 200 kilograms, and an African elephant weighs 264 kilograms. By adulthood, both types of elephants will weigh close to four tons.

An elephant's ears weigh more than 45 kilograms each.

An elephant's trunk is strong enough to tear a tree out of the ground, nimble enough to untie a knot and sensitive enough to smell water three miles away.

To keep from damaging its skeleton, which is supporting as much weight as it can, an African elephant has to move sedately, never jumping or running. The 'charge' of these animals is a fast walk, at about 15 miles per hour.

Elephants greet returning members of their group by spinning around, flapping their ears and trumpeting.

Tusks grow throughout an elephant's life.

HISTORY

Each king in a deck of playing cards represents a king from history. The king of spades is King David, the king of clubs is Alexander the Great, the king of hearts is Charlemagne, and the king of diamonds is Julius Caesar.

Michelangelo's cook was illiterate so he drew her a shopping list - which still exists and is now priceless.

February 1865 is the only month in recorded history not to have a full moon.

Pirates wore earrings in the belief that it improved their eyesight.

Until the 19th century, blocks of tea were used as money in Siberia.

In the 13th century, the Pope set quality standards for pasta.

In 1883, the eruption of Krakatoa put so much dust into the atmosphere that all around the world for the next two years sunsets appeared green and the Moon appeared blue.

The ancient Egyptians used to bury mummified mice with their mummified cats.

In 1915, William Wrigley Jr sent chewing gum to everyone in the phone book.

Pepi II, of Egypt, was the longest-ruling king in history. He was king for 94 years, from the age of six until he died at the age of 100.

When the Black Death swept across Europe in the 14th century, it was a long time before the true cause was understood. One theory was that cats caused the plague, and so thousands were slaughtered. This made the problem worse. The cats had been helping keep houses clear of the real culprits: rats. Over five years, 25 million people died of the plague in Europe.

The gold earrings many sailors wore were to pay for a decent burial on their death.

The Chinese have used fingerprints as a method of identification for 1,500 years.

Apollo 11, which landed on the Moon in 1969, had 36 seconds' worth of fuel left when it returned.

'BEST IN SHOW' AT CRUFTS

2010: Hungarian Vizsla
2009: Sealyham Terrier
2008: Giant Schnauzer
2007: Tibetan Terrier
2006: Australian Shepherd
2005: Norfolk Terrier
2004: Whippet
2003: Pekingese
2002: Standard Poodle
2001: Basenji
2000: Kerry Blue Terrier
1999: Irish Setter
1998: Welsh Terrier
1997: Yorkshire Terrier
1996: Cocker Spaniel
1995: Irish Setter
1994: Welsh Terrier
1993: Irish Setter
1992: Whippet
1991: Clumber Spaniel

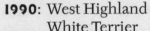

1990: West Highland White Terrier
1989: Bearded Collie
1988: English Setter
1987: Afghan Hound
1986: Airedale Terrier
1985: Standard Poodle
1984: Lhasa Apso
1983: Afghan Hound
1982: Toy Poodle
1981: Irish Setter
1980: Retriever (Flat Coated)
1979: Kerry Blue Terrier

1978: Wire Fox Terrier

1977: English Setter

1976: West Highland White Terrier

1975: Wire Fox Terrier

1974: St Bernard

1973: Cavalier King Charles Spaniel

1972: Bull Terrier

1971: German Shepherd

1970: Pyrenean Mountain

1969: Alsatian

1968: Dalmatian

1967: Lakeland Terrier

1966: Toy Poodle

1965: Alsatian

1964: English Setter

1963: Lakeland Terrier

1962: Wire Fox Terrier

1961: Airedale Terrier

1960: Irish Wolfhound

1959: Welsh Terrier

1958: Pointer

1957: Keeshond

1956: Greyhound

1955: Standard Poodle

1954: *show cancelled*

1953: Great Dane

1952: Bulldog

1951: Welsh Terrier

1950: Cocker Spaniel

1949: *no show*

1948: Cocker Spaniel

1940–1947: *no shows*

1939: Cocker Spaniel

1938: Cocker Spaniel

1937: Retriever (Labrador)

1936: Chow Chow

1935: Pointer

1934: Greyhound

1933: Retriever (Labrador)

1932: Retriever (Labrador)

1931: Cocker Spaniel

1930: Cocker Spaniel

1929: Scottish Terrier

1928: Greyhound

HOW TO PLAY CRICKET

When both sides have been in and all the men are out (including those who are not out), then the game is finished.

When they are all out, the side that's out comes in and the side that's been in goes out and tries to get those coming in, out.

When a man goes out to go in, the men who are out try to get him out, and when he is out he goes in and the next man in goes out and goes in.

Each man that's in the side that's in goes out, and when he's out he comes in and the next man goes in until he's out.

Sometimes, there are men still in and not out.

There are two men called umpires who stay out all the time and they decide when the men who are in are out.

You have two sides, one out in the field and one in.

COUNTRIES THAT DRIVE ON THE LEFT

United Kingdom, South Africa, Australia, Sri Lanka, Mauritius, Nepal, Cyprus, India, Lesotho, Indonesia, Singapore, Bangladesh, Namibia, Surinam, Pakistan, Uganda, Fiji, Barbados, Japan, Malaysia, the Seychelles, Brunei, the Bahamas, the British Virgin Islands, Kenya, Tanzania, Papua New Guinea, Swaziland, Mozambique, Zambia, Guyana, Malta, Ireland, Jamaica, Thailand, Malawi, New Zealand, Nauru, Botswana, Trinidad and Tobago, Dominica, Grenada, St Lucia, Western Samoa, St Vincent, Zimbabwe

ALL THE CLUBS THAT HAVE LEFT THE FOOTBALL LEAGUE (WITHOUT BEING READMITTED)

Aberdare Athletic	1927
Ashington	1929
Barrow	1972
Bootle	1893
Bradford Park Avenue	1970
Burton United	1907
Chester City	2000
Darwen	1899
Durham City	1928
Gainsborough Trinity	1912
Gateshead	1960
Glossop	1915
Leeds City	1919

Loughborough	1900
Maidstone United	1992
Merthyr Town	1930
Middlesbrough Ironopolis	1894
Nelson	1931
New Brighton	1951
New Brighton Tower	1901
Newport County	1988
Northwich Victoria	1894
Scarborough	1999
Stalybridge Celtic	1923
Thames	1932
Wigan Borough	1931
Workington	1977

AMPHIBIANS

Bullfrogs pretend to be dead if captured, but then quickly hop away if the captor releases its grip.

Some frogs can be frozen solid then thawed and still be alive.

Amphibians see only in black and white. Their eyes come in a variety of shapes and sizes, and some have square or heart-shaped pupils.

A single toad can eat 10,000 insects in the course of a summer.

Toads have dry 'warty' skin, dull-coloured fat bodies and poison glands behind the eyes. They walk or waddle, while frogs hop.

Frogs and toads never eat with their eyes open because they have to push food down into their stomach with the back of their eyeballs.

Frogs don't drink water – they absorb it through their skin.

Alpine salamanders always give birth to twins.

When a horned toad is angry, it squirts blood from its eyes.

Lungless salamanders
– the largest group of
salamanders
– breathe through
their skin, which
must be kept damp
to allow oxygen
in. If they dry out,
they suffocate and
die.

**The
Ozark
blind
salamander
begins life with eyes. As the
animal matures, its eyelids fuse together.**

Frogs have teeth but toads don't.

Toads only eat prey that moves.

The Argentinian horned toad can swallow a
mouse in one gulp.

DISHES FROM AROUND THE WORLD

Pig's Organs in Blood Sauce (**Philippines**)

Baked Bat (**Samoa**)

Crispy Roasted Termites (**Swaziland**)

Roast Field Mice (**Mexico**)

Weaver Moths in Their Nests (**Zaire**)

Parrot Pie (actually 12 budgerigars) (**Australia**)

Bee Grubs in Coconut Cream (**Thailand**)

Guinea Pig in a Creole Style (**Peru**)

Queen White Ants (**South Africa**)

Calf Udder Croquettes (**France**)

Coconut Cream-marinated Dog (**Indonesia**)

Mice in Cream (**Arctic**)

Starling Stew with Olives (**Turkey**)

Stewed Cane Rat (**Ghana**)

Water Beetle Cocktail Sauce (**Laos**)

Turtle Ragout (**Mexico**)

Stuffed Bear's Paw (**Romania**)

Red Ant Chutney (**India**)

Baked Muskrat (**Canada**)

Raw Octopus (**Hawaii**)

Calf's Lung and Heart in a
Paprika Sauce (**Hungary**)

Fox Tongues (**Japan**)

Pig's Face (**Ireland**)

Silkworm Pupae Soup (**Vietnam**)

Cajun Squirrel Ravioli (**US**)

Turtle Casserole (**Fiji**)

Lambs' Tails and Honey (**Morocco**)

Sun-dried Maggots (**China**)

CAPITAL CITIES – AND WHAT THEIR NAMES MEAN

NAME	COUNTRY	MEANING
Khartoum	Sudan	elephant's trunk
Bangkok	Thailand	wild-plum village
Buenos Aires	Argentina	good winds
Montevideo	Uruguay	I saw the mountain
Kuala Lumpur	Malaysia	mud-yellow estuary
Brussels	Belgium	buildings on a marsh
Freetown	Sierra Leone	town for liberated slaves
Seoul	South Korea	the capital
Sofia	Bulgaria	wisdom
Tehran	Iran	warm place

THE 10 YOUNGEST POPSTARS WITH (SOLO) NUMBER-ONE HITS

⭐ **Little Jimmy Osmond** (9 years, 8 months old)
'Long-haired Lover From Liverpool' 1972

⭐ **Donny Osmond** (14 years, 6 months old)
'Puppy Love' 1972

⭐ **Helen Shapiro** (14 years, 10 months old)
'You Don't Know' 1961

⭐ **Billie Piper** (15 years, 9 months old)
'Because We Want To' 1998

⭐ **Paul Anka** (16 years, 0 months old)
'Diana' 1957

⭐ **Tiffany** (16 years, 3 months old)
'I Think We're Alone Now' 1987

⭐ **Nicole** (17 years old)
'A Little Peace' 1982

⭐ **Britney Spears** (17 years, 2 months old)
'. . . Baby One More Time' 1999

⭐ **Sandie Shaw** (17 years, 7 months old)
'Always Something There to Remind Me' 1964

⭐ **Gareth Gates** (17 years, 9 months old)
'Unchained Melody' 2002

⭐ **Glen Madeiros** (18 years old)
'Nothing's Gonna Change My Love' 1988

ONLYs

The bloodhound is the **ONLY** animal whose evidence is admissible in an American court.

Monday is the ONLY day of the week that has an anagram: dynamo.

Libra (the scales) is the **ONLY** inanimate symbol in the zodiac.

The ONLY rock that floats in water is pumice.

Malayalam, spoken in Kerala, southern India, is the **ONLY** language with a palindromic name – which means it reads the same backwards.

A person from the country of Nauru is called a Nauruan; this is the ONLY palindromic nationality.

'Subbookkeeper' is the **ONLY** word found in an English dictionary with four pairs of double letters in a row.

'Forty' is the ONLY number with its letters in alphabetical order.

A Dalmatian is the **ONLY** dog that can get gout.

'One' is the **ONLY** number with its letters in reverse alphabetical order.

If there were an ocean big enough, Saturn would be the ONLY planet that could float because its density is lighter than that of water (it is mostly gas).

Your tongue is the **ONLY** muscle in your body that is attached at only one end.

The ONLY bone never yet broken in a skiing accident is one located in the inner ear.

Hummingbirds are the **ONLY** birds able to fly backwards.

Christopher Lee was the ONLY member of the cast (and crew) of the *Lord of the Rings* movies to have met the writer, J. R. R. Tolkien.

Earth is the **ONLY** planet not named after a god.

New Zealand is the ONLY country that has every type of climate in the world.

Black lemurs are the **ONLY** primates, other than humans, that can have blue eyes.

Europe is the ONLY continent without a desert.

Nauru is the ONLY country in the world with no official capital.

The letter W is the ONLY letter in the alphabet that has three – rather than one – syllables.

Pecans are the ONLY food that astronauts can take untreated into space.

Venus is the ONLY planet that rotates clockwise.

Canada is the ONLY country not to win a gold medal in the summer Olympic Games while hosting the event.

The **ONLY** living tissue in the human body that contains no blood vessels is the transparent cornea of the eye.

The polar bear is the ONLY mammal with hair on the soles of its feet.

Salt is the ONLY rock humans can eat.

Honey is the ONLY natural food that doesn't spoil.

The San Francisco cable cars are the ONLY mobile national monuments in the US.

Texas is the ONLY US state that permits residents to vote from space.

Humans, ants and, to a lesser degree, chimpanzees are the ONLY beings that wage war.

The ONLY dog in a Shakespeare play is Crab, in *The Two Gentlemen of Verona*.

Madrid (Spain) and Valetta (Malta) are the ONLY European capital cities not on rivers.

Devon is the ONLY county in Britain to have two coasts.

CELEBRITIES AND THE FOOTBALL TEAMS THEY SUPPORT

Matt Lucas	**Arsenal**
Orlando Bloom	**West Ham United**
Jarvis Cocker	**Sheffield Wednesday**
Zoe Ball	**Manchester United**
Hugh Grant	**Fulham**
Nigel Kennedy	**Aston Villa**
Robson Green	**Newcastle United**
Elijah Wood	**West Ham United**
Nicky Campbell	**Hearts**
Michael Palin	**Sheffield Wednesday**
Catherine Zeta-Jones	**Swansea City**
Robbie Williams	**Port Vale**
Noel and Liam Gallagher	**Manchester City**

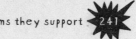

Sir Richard Branson	Aston Villa
Ant and Dec	Newcastle United
Kevin Costner	Arsenal
Prince William	Aston Villa
Dido	Arsenal
Phillip Schofield	Cardiff City
Mike Myers	Liverpool
Steve Coogan	Manchester United
Geri Halliwell	Watford
Martin Clunes	QPR
Rachel Stevens	Arsenal
Lucy Liu	Manchester United
Jenny Frost	Liverpool
Tony McCoy	Arsenal
Bill Nighy	Crystal Palace
Keira Knightley	West Ham

BEFORE FAME

Billie Piper made her TV debut impersonating Posh Spice.

Noel Gallagher used to be a roadie for the Inspiral Carpets (and Liam got the name Oasis from an Inspiral Carpets poster).

Michael Crawford took his stage name off a biscuit tin.

Catherine Zeta-Jones broke into showbusiness as a teenage Shirley Bassey impersonator.

Geena Davis has an elbow that bends the wrong way (and when she was young, she'd do things like stand in a lift and the doors would close and she'd pretend that her arm had got caught).

Matt Damon used to break-dance for money in Harvard Square.

Paul Bettany used to busk on Westminster Bridge.

Nathan Lane used to work as a singing telegram.

Minnie Driver attended finishing schools in Paris and Grenoble.

At one point, **Jim Carrey** and his family lived out of their car and trailer.

Colin Farrell auditioned for Boyzone but didn't get in.

ACHIEVEMENTS BEFORE THE AGE OF 10

✪ At the age of three, the 19th-century English philosopher **John Stuart Mill** was able to read Greek.

✪ At the age of four, **Lulu** sang in public for the first time.

✪ At the age of five, **Natalie Wood** appeared in her first film.

✪ At the age of five, **Tori Amos** won a scholarship to study the piano.

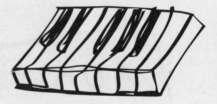

✪ At the age of six, **Shirley Temple** was awarded an honorary Oscar 'in grateful recognition of her outstanding contribution to screen entertainment during the year 1934'.

✪ At the age of seven, **Fred Astaire** was performing in vaudeville.

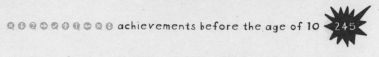
✪ At the age of eight, **Jamie Oliver** was cooking
in his father's pub.

✪ At the age of nine, **Macaulay Culkin** was cast
as the lead character in *Home Alone*, the film
that made him famous.

✪ At the age of nine, **Ruth Lawrence** passed
A-level maths.

GEOGRAPHY

Finland has more islands than any other country: 179,584.

Parsley is the most widely used herb in the world.

The Coca-Cola company is the largest consumer of sugar and vanilla in the world.

In Albania nodding the head means 'no' and shaking the head means 'yes'.

Eskimos use refrigerators to keep their food from freezing.

Approximately 20 per cent of Americans have passports.

Everything weighs one per cent less at the equator.

The people of Iceland read more books than any other people in the world.

Every gallon of seawater contains more than 100 grams of salt.

Two thirds of the world's aubergines are grown in New Jersey.

Birmingham has 22 more miles of canal than Venice.

More redheads are born in Scotland than in any other part of the world.

Canada has more lakes than the rest of the world combined.

10 per cent of the salt mined in the world each year is used to de-ice the roads in America.

One third of all the fresh water on Earth is in Canada.

One third of the world's land surface is desert.

28 per cent of Africa is wilderness; 38 per cent of North America is wilderness.

The surface of the Dead Sea is 400 metres below the surface of the Mediterranean Sea.

The African baobab tree is pollinated by bats and its blossom opens only to moonlight.

TONGUE TWISTERS

- Six sharp smart sharks.

- **The sixth sick sheik's sixth sheep's sick.**

- If Stu chews shoes, should Stu choose the shoes he chews?

- **Rory the warrior and Roger the worrier were wrongly reared in a rural brewery.**

- Black-back bat.

- **Sheena leads, Sheila needs.**

- A big black bug bit a big black bear, made the big black bear bleed blood.

- Lesser leather never weathered wetter weather better.

- **Scissors sizzle, thistles sizzle.**

- Wunwun was a racehorse, Tutu was one too. Wunwun won one race, Tutu won one too.

- **A box of biscuits, a batch of mixed biscuits.**

- The local yokel yodels.

- **Eleven benevolent elephants.**

- Red lorry, yellow lorry, red lorry, yellow lorry.

- **Is this your sister's sixth zither, sir?**

- **We shall surely see the sun shine soon.**

- A noisy noise annoys an oyster.

- **Three free throws.**

- Mrs Smith's Fish Sauce Shop.

- **Black bug's blood.**

- Friendly Frank flips fine flapjacks.

- **Six slick slim sick sycamore saplings.**

- Fred fed Ted bread and Ted fed Fred bread.

- **Selfish shellfish.**

- Cheap ship trip.

- **How much wood would a woodchuck chuck if a woodchuck could chuck wood?**

- **Six slippery snails slid slowly seaward.**

- Irish wristwatch.

- **Peter Piper picked a peck of pickled peppers. Did Peter Piper pick a peck of pickled peppers? If Peter Piper picked a peck of pickled peppers, where's the peck of pickled peppers Peter Piper picked?**

THE CHANCE OF . . .

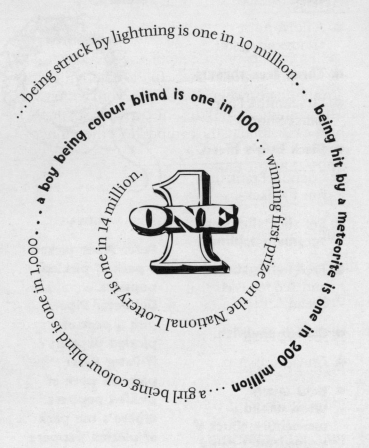

. . . being struck by lightning is one in 10 million . . . being hit by a meteorite is one in 200 million . . . a girl being colour blind is one in 14 million . . . winning first prize on the National Lottery is one in 14 million . . . a boy being colour blind is one in 100 . . . being colour blind is one in 1,000 . . .

ONE

THE WINNING WORD IN SOME OF THE US NATIONAL SPELLING BEES

Every year, the United States holds a national spelling competition. School pupils qualify for it by winning regional heats. In the final, children are eliminated when they spell a word wrong. The winning word is the one correctly spelled by the last child in the competition: the winner.

2009: LAODICEAN

2007: SERREFINE

2005: APPOGGIATURA

1995: XANTHOSIS

1985: MILIEU

1975: INCISOR

1965: ECZEMA

1955: CRUSTACEOLOGY

1946: SEMAPHORE

ASTRONOMY

✸ **The Sun is 93 million miles from Earth, which is 270 times closer than the next nearest star.**

✸ A car travelling at 100 miles per hour would take 106 years to reach the Sun.

✸ **It would take about 2,000 years to walk to the Sun.**

✸ It takes 8 minutes 12 seconds for sunlight to reach Earth.

✸ **If you think of the Milky Way as being the size of Asia, then our solar system would be the size of a penny.**

✸ The Earth travels 12 million miles a day.

✸ **Footprints left on the Moon by astronauts will remain visible for at least 10 million years.**

✸ A lightning bolt is five times hotter than the surface of the Sun.

✸ **Over 1,000 planets the size of the Earth could fit inside the Sun.**

✸ Uranus is visible to the naked eye.

- If you were standing on Mercury, the Sun would appear two and a half times larger than it appears on Earth.

- **The Milky Way galaxy contains five billion stars that are larger than our Sun.**

- The Earth weighs approximately 6,588,000,000,000,000,000 tons.

- **10 tons of space dust falls on the Earth every day.**

- When the Americans sent a man into space, they spent a million dollars developing a pen that could write upside down in conditions of zero gravity. The Russians used a pencil.

- **A modern PC is more powerful than all of NASA's computers at the time of the Apollo moon landings (1969) put together.**

- A day on Jupiter is approximately 9 hours, 50 minutes and 30 seconds long at the equator.

- **Average wind speed on Jupiter is 225 miles per hour.**

- The volume of the Moon and the volume of the Pacific Ocean are the same.

❊ **Most stars shine for at least 10 billion years.**

❊ The Earth is the densest planet in the solar system.

❊ **A manned rocket reaches the Moon in less time than it once took a stagecoach to travel the length of England.**

❊ The winds on Saturn blow at 1,200 miles per hour – 10 times faster than a strong Earth hurricane.

❊ **The number of UFO sightings increases when Mars is nearest Earth.**

❊ Every 11 years the magnetic poles of the Sun switch, in a cycle called 'solar maximum'.

❊ **Astronauts can't burp in space: there's no gravity to separate liquid from gas in their stomachs.**

❊ While astronauts might feel upset in space, lack of gravity will prevent their tears from rolling down their face.

ONLY IN BRITAIN

Only in Britain . . . do banks leave both doors open and chain the pens to the counters.

Only in Britain . . . were 142 men injured in a single year because they didn't remove all the pins from new shirts.

Only in Britain . . . are 58 people injured every year by using sharp knives instead of screwdrivers.

Only in Britain . . . are more than 200 people a year admitted to A&E after opening bottles of beer with their teeth.

Only in Britain . . . do people order double cheeseburgers, large fries and a Diet Coke.

Only in Britain . . . do chemists make ill people walk all the way to the back of the store to get their prescriptions while healthy people can buy chocolate bars at the front.

NUMBER 142,857

When 142,857 is multiplied by any number from 1 to 6, the result is a number containing the same digits in the same order – but starting in a different place.

1 x 142,857 = 142,857
2 x 142,857 = 285,714
3 x 142,857 = 428,571
4 x 142,857 = 571,428
5 x 142,857 = 714,285
6 x 142,857 = 857,142

Look what happens when you multiply 142,857 by 7: it equals 999,999.

When 1 is divided by 7 it comes to 0.142857,142857,142857.

If you multiply 142,857 by 8, you get 1142856.
If you take off the first digit (1) and add it to
the remaining six digits, see what happens:
1 + 142856 = 142857.

Similarly, if you multiply 142,857 by - say
- 17, you get 2,428,569. Now take off the
first digit (2) and add it to the remaining six
digits and see what happens: 2 + 428,569
= 428,571 - which is, of course, the original
number in stage three of its cycle.

You can do this with every number except
multiples of 7 (although these also produce
interesting results).

If you take the number 142,857 and split it
into two - 142 and 857 - and then add those
two numbers, you get 999.

SHARKS

- **The nurse shark spends much of its time in caves.**

- The white shark is the only sea creature with no natural enemies.

- **A shark is the only fish that can blink with both eyes.**

- A shark can grow a new set of teeth in a week.

- **One species of shark is so competitive that the babies fight each other within the womb, until only one is left to be born alive.**

- Sharks are older than dinosaurs, as shown by their fossil records.

- **Many sharks lay soft-shelled eggs but hammerhead sharks give birth to live young that are miniature versions of their parents. Young hammerheads emerge head first, with the tip of their hammerhead folded back to make the birth easier.**

FISH

The fastest fish in the sea is the swordfish, which can reach speeds of 68 miles per hour.

Bluefin tuna can swim at 50 miles per hour.

Five piranha fish could chew a horse and rider up in seven minutes.

Fish can drown if there isn't enough oxygen in the water, which can happen if the water is polluted.

THE QUEEN

The Queen was the first future monarch to be born in a private house – 17 Bruton Street, London W1 – which is now the site of a bank. When she was born, she was third in line to the throne. Her father and her uncle David, later King Edward VIII, were ahead of her.

She learned to curtsey perfectly before the age of two and made her last curtsey in 1952, to her father's body in St George's Chapel, Windsor.

She and Prince Philip were related before they married. They're third cousins (through their descent from Queen Victoria) and second cousins once removed (through King Christian IX of Denmark).

The Queen has only once signed an autograph for a member of the public. In 1945, Sergeant Pat Hayes asked for her autograph and was given it.

Her childhood nickname was 'Lilibet', which was the way she mispronounced her own name. This is still the name her closest relatives call her. Queen Mary, her grandmother, called her 'the bambino'.

At the precise moment in 1952 when she acceded to the throne, she was wearing a shirt, a cardigan and a pair of trousers.

She is superstitious. She throws salt over her left shoulder if she accidentally spills any, she won't have 13 people at the dinner table and she's been known to touch wood before her horses run.

Whenever she travels abroad she always takes with her barley water, a specially formulated egg and lemon shampoo and her feather pillow.

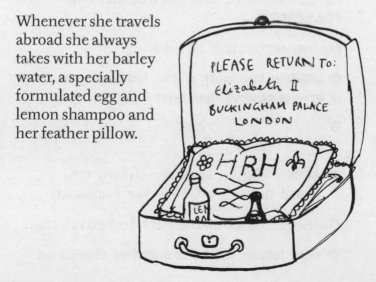

PLEASE RETURN TO:
Elizabeth II
BUCKINGHAM PALACE
LONDON

HRH

LEM ON

THE QUEEN LOVES: military march music, popular classical works and musicals, champagne, corgis, watching TV, horse racing, crossword puzzles, impersonations (she's a gifted impressionist herself) and charades.

AS QUEEN, SHE CAN DO ALL OF THE FOLLOWING:

- drive without taking a driving test

- disobey the laws of the land because they are, of course, her laws

- refuse to give evidence in court as the courts are her courts

- declare war on another country (the armed forces are under her command)

- disband the army and sell all the navy's ships

- send letters without putting stamps on

- give as many honours – including peerages and knighthoods – as she likes

- **dismiss the government**

- pardon any (or all) of the prisoners in her jails

- **get rid of the Civil Service**

THE QUEEN'S RETINUE INCLUDES:
Keeper of the Queen's Swans, Mistress of the Robes, Queen's Raven Master, Clerk of the Closet, Lady of the Bedchamber, Woman of the Bedchamber, Hereditary Grand Falconer, Royal Bargemaster, Queen's Racing Pigeon Manager and Grand Almoner.

THE QUEEN HATES: dictating letters, garlic, cats, tennis, pomposity, the cold, smoking, and any mention of King Edward VIII, whose abdication pushed her father on to the throne.

THE WAY WE LIVE

The average driver gets locked out of his or her car nine times.

One in 10 people in the world live on an island.

AND I'M JUST SHOWING OFF!

THE SHOW-OFF

Next time you see a statue in a park of someone on a horse, look at the horse's legs. If the horse has both front legs in the air, the person on the horse died in battle. If the horse has one front leg in the air, the person died as a result of wounds received in battle. If the horse has all four legs on the ground, the person died of natural causes.

90 per cent of people turn right on walking into a department store. No one knows why.

More work gets done on a Tuesday than on any other day.

The original purpose of the tablecloth was as a towel on which to wipe fingers and faces after eating.

The melting point of cocoa butter is just below body temperature – that's why chocolate melts in your mouth.

In China, the bride wears red.

In most of the world's languages, the word for 'mother' begins with the letter 'm'.

Mexico City has more taxis than any other city in the world.

85 per cent of international phone calls are conducted in English.

In the course of a lifetime, we spend about two years on the phone, and eat about 35,000 biscuits (not necessarily at the same time).

When asked for a colour, three out of five people say red.

17,000 individual Smarties are eaten every minute in the UK.

Peanuts are one of the ingredients of dynamite.

People spend more than five years of their lives dreaming.

There is no such thing as naturally blue food – even blueberries are purple.

The QWERTY keyboard was designed so that the left hand typed the most common letters. This was to slow typists down (the right-handed ones at least) because early keyboards were prone to jamming.

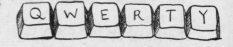

The three primary colours are red, yellow and blue.

The three secondary colours, which you get from mixing two primary colours, are green, orange and purple.

Fingerprints provide traction for the fingers.

We forget 80 per cent of what we learn every day.

There are 4.3 births and 1.7 deaths in the world every second.

There are more mobile phones than people in Britain.

Only a third of the people who can twitch their ears can twitch them one at a time.

71 per cent of office workers stopped on the street for a survey agreed to give up their computer passwords in exchange for a chocolate bar.

One in every four Americans has appeared on television.

We reach the peak of our ability to see ghosts at the age of seven.

night ghostie

A computer user blinks about seven times a minute.

If all the Easter eggs sold in Britain in one year were laid end to end, they'd go from London to Australia and halfway back again.

If you are struck by lightning once, you are 100,000 times more likely to get struck again.

The average age in Britain is 38 years.

Laughing lowers levels of stress and strengthens the immune system.

CREEPY CRAWLIES

- Termites do more damage in the US every year than all the fires, storms and earthquakes combined.

- **A mosquito has 47 teeth.**

- The average caterpillar has 2,000 muscles in its body (we have 656).

- **Tarantulas can go for up to two years without eating.**

- Snails can sleep and not eat for three years.

- **Queen bees only ever use their stingers to kill other queen bees.**

- Queen termites can live for up to 100 years.

- **The ant can lift 50 times its own weight and can pull 30 times its own weight.**

- The praying mantis is the only insect that can turn its head without moving its body.

- **Mother tarantulas kill 99 per cent of the babies they hatch.**

The only food cockroaches won't eat is cucumber.

The snail is the only insect with retractable antennae.

The housefly hums in the note of F.

The most poisonous spider is not the black widow but the wingless daddy longlegs – but its fangs can't pierce human skin and so it poses no threat.

The flea can jump 350 times its body length.

Gram for gram, a bumblebee is 150 times stronger than an elephant.

An ant can survive for two weeks underwater.

Anteaters prefer eating termites to ants.

ANIMALS

A sloth can move twice as fast in water as it can on land.

Reindeer like bananas.

A tiger's night vision is six times better than ours.

Racehorses have been known to wear out new shoes in one race.

At top speed a pig can run a mile in 7.5 minutes.

Koalas rarely drink water, but get fluids from the eucalyptus leaves they eat. In fact, 'koala' is believed to mean 'no drink' in the Aboriginal language.

The pocket gopher, a burrowing rodent, can run backwards as fast as it can run forwards.

A laboratory mouse runs five miles per night on its treadmill.

Bulls and crocodiles are colour-blind.

A mole can dig 75 metres of tunnel in a single night.

A cow gives nearly 200,000 glasses of milk in her lifetime.

Cows can smell odours six miles away.

Reindeer have scent glands between their hind toes. The glands help them leave cheesy-smelling scent trails for the herd to follow.

Sloths spend 75 per cent of their lives asleep.

A Holstein's spots are unique – no two cows have the same pattern of spots.

A dairy cow produces four times its weight in manure each year.

Armadillos can be house-trained.

A full-grown bear can run as fast as a horse.

Deer sleep for only five minutes a day.

The fastest animal on four legs is the cheetah, which races at speeds of up to 70 miles per hour. It can reach 45 miles per hour in two seconds.

Kangaroo means 'I don't understand' in Aborigine.

A polar bear's skin is black. Its fur is not white, but clear.

There are more kangaroos than people in Australia.

Denmark has twice as many pigs as people.

A rat can fall from a five-storey building without hurting itself.

A rhinoceros's horn is made of compacted hair.

Brazil, Argentina, Australia and New Zealand all have more cattle than people.

Mice will nurse babies that are not their own.

The orangutan's warning signal to would-be aggressors is a loud belch.

The woolly mammoth had tusks almost five metres long.

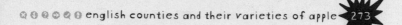

ENGLISH COUNTIES AND THEIR VARIETIES OF APPLE

♂ **Kent:** Kentish Fillbasket, Mabbott's Pearmain, Gascoyne's Scarlet, Golden Knob ♂ **Yorkshire:** Green Balsam, Flower of the Town, French Crab, Acklam Russett ♂ **Hereford:** King's Acre Pippin, Herefordshire Beefing, Lord Hindlip, Yellow Ingestrie ♂ **Lancashire:** Golden Spire, Roseberry, Scotch Bridget, Proctor's Seedling ♂ **Surrey:** Claygate Pearmain, Cockles Pippin, George Carpenter, Joybells, Scarlet Nonpareil ♂ **Devon:** Michaelmas Stubbard, Crimson Costard, Devonshire Quarrenden, Star of Devon ♂ **Sussex:** Crawley Beauty, Forge, Lady Sudeley, First and Last, Wadhurst Pippin ♂ **Hertfordshire:** Lane's Prince Albert, Golden Reinette, Bushey Grove ♂ **Cornwall:** Cornish Gilliflower, Glass Apple, Cornish Pine, Tommy Knight

PURE TRIVIA

More grapes are grown than any other fruit.

Nanotechnology has produced a guitar no bigger than a blood cell. The guitar, 10 micrometres long, has strings that can be strummed.

Abraham Lincoln's Gettysburg Address was just 267 words long.

South Africa used to have two official languages. Now it has 11.

Huge wine jugs were often used by the ancient Greeks as coffins.

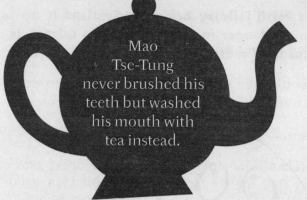

Mao
Tse-Tung
never brushed his
teeth but washed
his mouth with
tea instead.

A metal coat hanger is 112 centimetres long when straightened.

Rubber bands last longer when refrigerated.

The Basque language, one of Europe's oldest, is not derived from any other language.

Nintendo was established in 1889 and started out making playing cards.

The mongoose was brought to Hawaii to kill rats but the project failed – rats are nocturnal while the mongoose hunts during the day.

Himalaya means 'home of snow'.

The Forth railway bridge in Scotland is up to a metre longer in summer than in winter. It is made of metal, which expands in the heat.

It would take about two million hydrogen atoms to cover the full stop at the end of this sentence.

Jellyfish are 95 per cent water.

The model ape used in the 1933 film *King Kong* was 46 centimetres tall.

Johann Sebastian Bach once walked 230 miles to hear the organist at Lübeck in Germany.

There are two independent nations in Europe smaller than New York's Central Park: Vatican City and Monaco.

As a young and struggling artist, Pablo Picasso kept warm by burning his own paintings.

There is more sugar in one kilogram of lemons than in one kilogram of strawberries.

About 70 per cent of all living things in the world are bacteria.

The yo-yo originated in the Philippines, where it was used as a weapon in hunting.

The board game Monopoly was originally rejected by Parker Brothers, who claimed it had 52 errors.

L. Frank Baum got the name Oz in *The Wizard of Oz* from one of his alphabetized filing cabinets (O–Z).

Cuckoo clocks come from the Black Forest in Germany – not Switzerland.

If you were locked in a completely sealed room, you'd die of carbon-dioxide poisoning rather than lack of oxygen.

The sound made by the Victoria Falls in Zimbabwe can be heard 40 miles away.

SEA LIFE

◀ An octopus can undo the lid of a screw-top jar.

◀ **The noise made by a pistol shrimp is so loud that it can shatter glass.**

◀ A lobster can lay 150,000 eggs at one time.

◀ **The giant squid is the largest creature without a backbone.**

◀ A sea urchin walks on its teeth.

◀ **The giant Pacific octopus can fit its entire body through an opening no bigger than the size of its beak.**

◀ Using its web – the skin between its arms – an octopus can carry up to a dozen crabs back to its den to eat.

◀ **The strictly correct plural of 'octopus' is 'octopodes', but 'octopuses' is much more commonly used.**

◀ Coral and jellyfish are closely related.

- **The sponge is an animal without a nervous system.**

- A baby oyster is called a spat.

- **If a lobster loses an eye, it can grow a new one.**

- Octopuses – sorry, 'octopodes' – have gardens.

- **Shrimps and eels can swim backwards as well as forwards.**

- Jellyfish sometimes evaporate if stranded on a beach.

- **The shrimp's heart is in its head.**

- Giant squid have tentacles as long as telegraph poles and eyes bigger than footballs. They have the largest eyes in the world.

- **Nine out of every 10 living things live in the ocean.**

USED TO BE BOY SCOUTS

Rolf Harris, Bill Clinton, Richard Gere, Neil Armstrong, President Jacques Chirac, Sir David Attenborough, Michael Parkinson, Sir Richard Branson, Sir Paul McCartney, Chris Tarrant

USED TO BE GIRL GUIDES

Björk, Emma Forbes, Emma Thompson, Ann Widdecombe, Mariah Carey, Venus Williams, Carol Vorderman, Cherie Blair, the Queen, Cat Deeley, Hillary Clinton

THE USA

- There are 556 officially recognized Native American tribes.

- **In Los Angeles, there are more cars than people.**

- Every hour, 12,500 puppies are born in the United States.

- **Deafness was once so common on Martha's Vineyard that all the people who lived there, both the hearing and the deaf, were fluent in sign language.**

- In Alaska, it is against the law to push a living moose out of a moving aeroplane.

- **In 1980, a Las Vegas hospital suspended workers for taking bets on when patients would die.**

- All the earthworms in America weigh 55 times what all the people weigh.

- **The largest living thing on Earth (by volume) is the General Sherman tree in Sequoia National Park. It is 84 metres tall and its trunk is 11 metres in diameter at the widest point.**

- **The United States has five per cent of the world's population, 25 per cent of the world's prisoners and 70 per cent of the world's lawyers.**

- In September 2004, a Minnesota state trooper issued a speeding ticket to a motorcyclist who was doing 205 miles per hour.

- **Since 1 January 2004, the population of the United States has been increasing by one person every 12 seconds. Every 13 seconds someone dies, every 8 seconds someone is born and every 25 seconds an immigrant arrives.**

- The United States consumes 25 per cent of the world's energy.

- **72 per cent of Americans sign their pets' names on the greetings cards they send.**

- Second Street is the most common street name in the United States.

- **Americans eat more bananas than any other fruit.**

- Every day, seven per cent of the US eats at McDonald's.

COUNTRIES THAT CHANGED THEIR NAMES

Rhodesia	to Zimbabwe
Upper Volta	to Burkina Faso
Aden	to Yemen
Abyssinia	to Ethiopia
Belgian Congo	to Zaire, and back to Congo
Dahomey	to Benin
Siam	to Thailand
Persia	to Iran
Basutoland	to Lesotho
British Honduras	to Belize
Gold Coast	to Ghana
Dutch Guiana	Surinam
Nyasaland	Malawi
The Afars and the Issas	Djibouti
Portuguese Guinea	Guinea-Bissau
Dutch East Indies	Indonesia
New Hebrides	Vanuatu
Bechuanaland	Botswana

CHRISTMAS

Christmas cards began in 15th-century Germany. In the mid-19th century, with the invention of the postage stamp, Christmas cards started to become popular in Britain.

The first ever Royal Christmas broadcast was made by King George V on the radio in 1932.

Christmas was officially abolished in England between 1642 and 1652 by the Puritans.

In the US state of Indiana, there is a town called Santa Claus where courses are held for department store Santas. Graduates become a BSc (Bachelor of Santa Clausing).

The most popular Christmas card is one depicting Santa Claus and his reindeer.

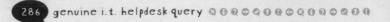

GENUINE I.T. HELPDESK QUERY

Customer: My keyboard is not working.

Helpdesk: Are you sure it's plugged into the computer?

Customer: No. I can't get behind the computer.

Helpdesk: Pick up your keyboard and walk 10 paces back.

Customer: OK.

Helpdesk: Did the keyboard come with you?

Customer: Yes.

Helpdesk: That means the keyboard is not plugged in.

THINGS SAID ABOUT SCHOOL

'Education
is what remains
after one has forgotten what
one has learned in school'
Albert Einstein

**'Everyone is in awe of the lion tamer
in a cage with half a dozen lions
– everyone but a school bus driver'**
Laurence Peter

'I won't say ours was a tough school, but
we had our own coroner. We used to
write essays like: What I'm going to
be if I grow up'
Lenny Bruce

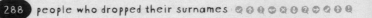
PEOPLE WHO DROPPED THEIR SURNAMES

Angelina Jolie
(Angelina Jolie Voight)

Richmal Crompton
(Richmal Crompton Lamburn)

David Blaine
(David Blaine White)

Tom Cruise
(Thomas Cruise Mapother IV)

WOMBATS

Wombats are nocturnal marsupials, found only in Australia.

Prince William was called Wombat as a child.

Wombats have a slow metabolism – it takes them 14 days to digest their food – and because of this they move slowly. However, they can run very fast if being chased.

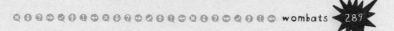

When being chased, a wombat can reach 25 miles per hour. It can then stop dead in half a stride. It kills its predators this way – the predator runs into the wombat's bum-bone and smashes its face.

It also uses its bum-bone to crush intruders against the wall of its burrow.

It would be illegal to keep a wombat as a pet.

Most Australians have never seen a wild wombat.

There are two kinds of wombat: the common wombat and the hairy-nosed wombat.

Wombats often sleep on their backs with their legs in the air, and they frequently snore.

BUNGEE JUMPERS

Davina McCall (over the Grand Canyon), Leonardo DiCaprio, Zara Phillips, Andre Agassi, Ian Wright, Jeremy Guscott, Stuart Barnes, Prince William, Robbie Williams, Orlando Bloom

PEOPLE WHO PLAYED FOR – OR HAD TRIALS WITH – FOOTBALL CLUBS

Bradley Walsh
(Brentford)

Rod Stewart
(Brentford)

Gordon Ramsay
(played twice for Rangers)

Audley Harrison
(Watford)

Ralf Little
(Swindon and Millwall)

Andrew Murray
(Rangers)

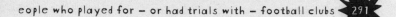

FAMOUS PEOPLE WITH A TWIN BROTHER/SISTER

Joseph Fiennes (Jake)
Vin Diesel (Paul)
Will Young (Rupert)
Kiefer Sutherland (Rachel)
Scarlett Johansson (Hunter)
Ashton Kutcher (Michael)
Simon Cowell (Nicholas)
Alanis Morissette (Wade)

FAMOUS TWINS

Mary-Kate and Ashley Olsen

FAMOUS COUSINS

Glenn Close & Brooke Shields
Imogen Stubbs & Alexander Armstrong
Joseph Fiennes & Sir Ranulph Fiennes
Christopher Lee and Ian Fleming
Madonna & Gwen Stefani (distant)
Oprah Winfrey & Elvis Presley (distant)

FAMOUS PEOPLE WHO ADOPTED CHILDREN

Tom Hanks, Angelina Jolie, Steven Spielberg, Walt Disney, Nicole Kidman & Tom Cruise, Calista Flockhart, Drew Barrymore, Dawn French, Dame Kiri Te Kanawa, Hugh Jackman

FAMOUS PEOPLE WHO HAD NO BROTHERS OR SISTERS

Shannon Elizabeth, Marilyn Manson, Craig David, Adrien Brody, Dale Winton, Teri Hatcher, Sarah Michelle Gellar, David Copperfield, David Gower, Robert De Niro, Charlotte Church, Chris Tarrant, Uri Geller, Sir Elton John, Harry Enfield

SCRABBLE

Scrabble was invented in 1931 by Alfred Butts, an unemployed American architect. Both the format and the name were changed many times before the current format was established with the name Scrabble in 1948.

Celebrity Scrabble fans include Brad Pitt, Norman Cook (Fatboy Slim), Jeremy Clarkson, Jonathan Ross, Ant, Dec, Chris Martin, Jennifer Aniston, Will Smith, Robbie Williams, Kylie Minogue, Madonna, Sting and Mel Gibson.

There are 109 permissible two-letter words. These include 'jo' (a sweetheart), 'ka' (a spirit), 'xi' (a letter in the Greek alphabet) and 'qi' (from the Chinese, it means 'life force').

Scrabble is made in 30 different languages.

The highest number of points that you can get in the first go (when there are no other letters on the board) is 126 – using the word SQUEEZY. Don't forget that there is a 50-point bonus for using all seven letters in one go.

In 1954, the game took off in Britain – selling 4.5 million sets. Today, about half the homes in Britain have a set.

SILLY SONG TITLES

'Hey, Young Fella, Close Your Old Umbrella'

'I'd Rather Be a Lobster Than a Wiseguy'

'(Potatoes Are Cheaper – Tomatoes Are Cheaper) Now's the Time to Fall in Love'

'All the Quakers Are Shoulder Shakers Down in Quaker Town'

'Come After Breakfast, Bring 'Long Your Lunch and Leave 'Fore Supper Time'

THE FUNNIEST JOKE IN THE WORLD . . . NOT

☺ In 2002, after much research, British scientists identified what they called **'The Funniest Joke in the World'**. Here it is:

☺ A couple of hunters are out in the woods when one of them falls to the ground. He doesn't seem to be breathing and his eyes are rolled back. The other man takes out his mobile phone and calls the emergency services. He says to the operator: **'My friend is dead! What can I do?'**

The operator, in a calm, soothing voice, says: **'Just take it easy. I can help. First, let's make sure he's dead.'**

There is a silence, then a shot is heard. The man's voice comes back on the line. He says: **'OK, now what?'**

Perhaps that just goes to show that there are some things you mustn't leave to scientists.

PANGRAMS

A pangram is a phrase or sentence that uses every single letter of the alphabet.

Xylophone wizard begets quick jive form.

Jackdaws love my big sphinx of quartz.

Quick wafting zephyrs vex bold Jim.

PALINDROMES

A palindrome is a word or sentence that reads the same backwards or forwards.

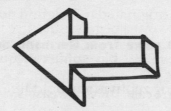

We panic in a pew.

Was it a car or a cat I saw?

Never odd or even.

Step on no pets.

Pull up if I pull up.

Madam, I'm Adam.

A nut for a jar of tuna.

Race fast, safe car.

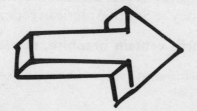

THINGS WHICH ARE NOT WHAT THEY SEEM

Rice paper contains no rice.

French fries originated in Belgium not France.

Great Danes come from Germany not Denmark.

Polecats aren't cats, they're weasels.

Koala bears aren't bears, they're marsupials.

Mountain goats aren't goats, they're small antelopes.

Fireflies aren't flies, they're beetles.

The funny bone isn't a bone, it's a nerve.

Jackrabbits aren't rabbits, they're hares.

Shooting stars aren't stars, they're meteors.

Prairie dogs aren't dogs, they're rodents.

Guinea pigs aren't pigs and nor are they from Guinea; they're South American rodents.

Lead pencils contain graphite, not lead.

Glow-worms aren't worms, they're beetles.

Horned toads aren't toads, they're lizards.

Bombay duck isn't duck, it's dried fish.

Silkworms aren't worms, they're caterpillars.

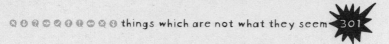

Peanuts aren't nuts, they're legumes.

There's no sand in sandpaper.

Black-eyed peas aren't peas, they're beans.

The French poodle originated in Germany.

The Jerusalem artichoke isn't an artichoke and doesn't come from Jerusalem. It's from America and is part of the sunflower family.

Bald eagles aren't bald. The top of the eagle's head is covered with slicked-down white feathers, which makes it look bald.

The Caspian Sea is a lake.

The grey whale is black.

Female blackbirds aren't black, they're brownish-grey.

The flying fox isn't a fox, it's a bat.

PURE TRIVIA

Rhinos are thought to have inspired the myth of the unicorn.

Mozart never went to school.

Cabbage is 91 per cent water.

There are more stars in the universe than grains of sand on all the beaches in the world.

The Snickers bar was named after a horse the Mars family owned.

The straw was invented by Egyptian brewers to taste beer during brewing without disturbing the fermenting matter floating on the top.

To get rid of warts, rub them with a peeled apple and then feed the apple to a pig. It's an old superstition but it might be worth a try.

Sylvester Stallone was kicked out of 14 schools in 11 years.

A group of geese on the ground is a gaggle; a group of geese in the air is a skein.

Sheep buried in snowdrifts can survive for up to two weeks.

Meat-eating animals will not eat the meat of an animal that has been hit by lightning.

Dalmatian dogs are born pure white and only get their spots when they're a few days old.

Chewing gum while peeling onions will keep you from crying.

During the Middle Ages, people tried to cure warts by putting spider webs on them.

Olympus Mons on Mars is the largest volcano in our solar system.

Windmills turn anti-clockwise.

A Boeing 767 airliner is made of 3,100,000 separate parts.

20 per cent of all road accidents in Sweden involve an elk.

Until the 18th century, India produced almost all the world's diamonds.

The steepest street in the world is Baldwin Street in Dunedin, New Zealand, with an incline of 38 per cent.

PEOPLE WHO HAVE BEEN PESTERED FOR AUTOGRAPHS IN TOILETS

Joan Collins stopped giving autographs after someone slid a piece of paper under a loo door and asked her to sign it.

Minnie Driver was also asked to give an autograph after someone slid a piece of paper under a loo door. She said, 'Could we do this outside?'

Sandi Toksvig was sitting in a public toilet that had a broken lock. A woman walked in by mistake and quickly went out again. Two seconds later, she came back and said, 'You're that Sandi Toksvig. Can I have your autograph?'

Julia Roberts was asked for an autograph while she was on the loo. She said, 'I'm the tiniest bit busy.'

Pierce Brosnan was asked while using a urinal. He obliged.

TOILET PAPER

Before the invention of toilet paper, people used shells or stones, bunches of herbs, or a bit of sponge attached to a stick which they rinsed with cold water.

The Victorians were so delicate they couldn't bring themselves to use the words 'toilet paper'. Instead they said 'curl papers'.

In 1986, Nathan Hicks of St Louis, Missouri, USA, shot his brother Herbert dead because he used six toilet rolls in two days.

LASTS

The guillotine was **LAST** used in France publicly in 1939 and non-publicly in 1977.

The LAST execution in the Tower of London took place on Thursday, 14 August 1941, when Josef Jakobs, a German spy, was shot by an eight-man firing squad.

When Thomas Edison died in 1941, Henry Ford captured his **LAST** dying breath in a bottle.

19.11.1999 was the LAST day when all the digits in the date were odd. There won't be another such date until 1.1.3111.

The **LAST** Olympics in which the gold medals were made entirely from gold were in 1912.

A wooden racket was LAST used at Wimbledon in 1987.

The **LAST** time a First Division/Premiership club had two players scoring more than 30 goals in a season was Sunderland in 1935–36, when Raich Carter and Bob Gurney each scored 31 goals.

The LAST letter George Harrison ever wrote was to Mike Myers asking for a Mini-Me doll.

LAST BREATH OF: Thomas Edison

THE UK ENTRIES IN THE EUROVISION SONG CONTEST
– and where they finished

YEAR	SONG	ARTIST	PLACE
2009	It's My Time	Jade Ewen	5th
2008	Even If	Andy Abraham	23rd
2007	Flying the Flag (For You)	Scooch	23rd
2006	Teenage Life	Daz Sampson	19th
2005	Touch My Fire	Javine	22nd
2004	Hold on to Our Love	James Fox	16th
2003	Cry Baby	Jemini	last with 'nul points'
2002	Come Back	Jessica Garlick	3rd
2001	No Dream Impossible	Lindsay D	15th
2000	Don't Play That Song Again	Nikki French	16th
1999	Say It Again	Precious	12th
1998	Where Are You?	Imaani	2nd
1997	Love Shine a Light	Katrina & the Waves	1st
1996	Ooh Aah Just a Little Bit	Gina G	8th
1995	Love City Groove	Love City Groove	joint 10th
1994	Lonely Symphony	Frances Ruffelle	10th
1993	Better the Devil You Know	Sonia	2nd

YEAR	SONG	ARTIST	PLACE
1992	One Step at a Time	Michael Ball	2nd
1991	A Message to Your Heart	Samantha Janus	10th
1990	Give a Little Love Back to the World	Emma Booth	6th
1989	Why Do I Always Get It Wrong?	Live Report	2nd
1988	Go	Scott Fitzgerald	2nd
1987	Only the Light	Rikki	13th
1986	Runner in the Night	Ryder	7th
1985	Love Is	Vikki Watson	4th
1984	Love Games	Belle and the Devotions	7th
1983	I'm Never Giving Up	Sweet Dreams	6th
1982	One Step Further	Bardo	7th
1981	Making Your Mind Up	Bucks Fizz	1st
1980	Love Enough for Two	Prima Donna	3rd
1979	Mary Anne	Black Lace	7th
1978	Bad Old Days	CoCo	11th
1977	Rock Bottom	Lynsey de Paul and Mike Moran	2nd
1976	Save Your Kisses for Me	The Brotherhood of Man	1st
1975	Let Me Be the One	The Shadows	2nd
1974	Long Live Love	Olivia Newton-John	4th

YEAR	SONG	ARTIST	PLACE
1973	Power to All My Friends	Cliff Richard	4th
1972	Beg, Steal or Borrow	The New Seekers	2nd
1971	Jack in the Box	Clodagh Rodgers	4th
1970	Knock, Knock, Who's There?	Mary Hopkin	2nd
1969	Boom Bang a Bang	Lulu	Joint 1st
1968	Congratulations	Cliff Richard	2nd
1967	Puppet on a String	Sandie Shaw	1st
1966	A Man Without Love	Kenneth McKellar	7th
1965	I Belong	Kathy Kirby	2nd
1964	I Love the Little Things	Matt Monro	2nd
1963	Say Wonderful Things	Ronnie Carroll	4th
1962	Ring-a-Ding Girl	Ronnie Carroll	4th
1961	Are You Sure?	The Allisons	2nd
1960	Looking High High High	Bryan Johnson	2nd
1959	Sing Little Birdie	Pearl Carr and Teddy Johnson	2nd
1958: No UK entry			
1957	All	Patricia Bredin	7th

FAMOUS LAST WORDS

'OK, I won't' Elvis Presley, after his girlfriend told him not to fall asleep in the bathroom, 1977

'That was a great game of golf, fellas' Bing Crosby, 1977

'Sir, I beg your pardon' Marie Antoinette, Queen of France, 1793, as she stepped on the executioner's foot

'KHAQQ calling Itasca. We must be on you, but cannot see you. Gas is running low' Amelia Earhart, 1937

FINALLY . . .

'I like long walks, especially when they are taken by people who annoy me' Fred Allen

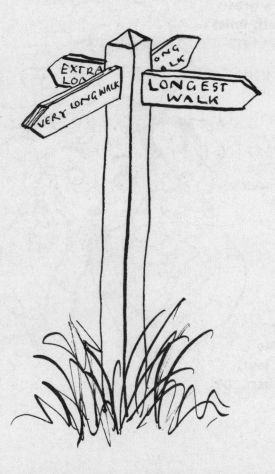